WINDOWS ME

in easy steps

HARSHAD KOTECHA

COMPUTER
STEP

In easy steps is an imprint of Computer Step
Southfield Road . Southam
Warwickshire CV47 OFB . England

http://www.ineasysteps.com

Notice of Liability

Every effort has been made to ensure that this book contains accurate
and current information. However, Computer Step and the author shall
not be liable for any loss or damage suffered by readers as a result of
any information contained herein.

Trademarks

Microsoft® and Windows® are registered trademarks of Microsoft
Corporation. All other trademarks are acknowledged as belonging to
their respective companies.

Printed and bound in the United Kingdom

ISBN 1-874029-94-6

Table Of Contents

First Steps

This chapter shows you how to start and shut down Windows ME. You'll learn how to use the Start button, and how to switch between different folder views. You'll also use the extensive online help system (including troubleshooters and support automation).

Covers

Chapter One

Introduction

Microsoft recommends that you use Windows 2000 Professional for business.

Microsoft Windows ME (or Millennium Edition) is designed specifically for home users. It is an upgrade of the following operating systems used on personal computers:

- MS-DOS
- Microsoft Windows for Workgroups 3.11
- Microsoft Windows 3.1, 95 and 98

Windows ME builds on features already incorporated into Windows 98. Some of the main innovations include:

- Enhanced Windows Media Player. You'll be able to play your favourite music CDs and video clips. You can also download music and other media content from the web, listen to Internet radio stations, create your own playlists and custom CDs.

- Windows Movie Maker. Create and edit your own home movies and then share them with friends and family over the Internet.

- Digital Photo Collection. Easily acquire pictures from a scanner or a digital camera and then build a photo album, create custom slide shows to send to friends, or simply use photos as wallpapers on your desktop.

- PC Gaming. Play better games faster and find online opponents more easily.

- Richer Internet Experience. Windows ME includes the latest Internet Explorer 5.5 browser software.

- Home Networking. If you have more than one computer in your home, then connect them easily to share files, printer, and the Internet connection.

- PC Health. This includes a number of improvements to make your PC more stable.

The basic foundation underlying any version of Windows is its 'windowing' capability. A window (spelt with a lower-case w) is a rectangular area used to display information or to run a program. Several windows can be opened at the same time to work with multiple applications, so you should be able to dramatically increase your productivity when using your computer.

Using your Mouse

Scroll More Easily

Zoom Efficiently

Raised Back Fits Your Hand

The wheel only works in software that has been specifically designed for it, like Microsoft Windows, Internet Explorer and Office.

A mouse is a pointing device used to communicate with your computer. The Microsoft IntelliMouse (as shown above) includes the standard two buttons plus a wheel sited between them. Use your index finger to operate the small wheel. This provides an extra level of speed and control when scrolling up and down documents or even web pages - it's much faster than clicking on the scroll arrows displayed. You can even use the wheel to zoom into images and text.

To use a mouse, first place it on a flat surface or use a mouse mat. You will notice an arrow-headed pointer (κ) moving on your screen as you move the mouse.

To make a selection, move the mouse pointer on top of an item and then press and release (or click) the left mouse button. Sometimes you can click twice in rapid succession (double-click) to open a folder, window, or a program.

You can set Windows to accept a

• single-click instead of the default double-click

• and simply rest the mouse pointer over an item for a few seconds to select it rather than clicking on it

See page 13 for further details.

A mouse will usually have at least one more button on the right (called the right mouse button). This provides further facilities – for example, a right-click of the mouse button when it is over an appropriate object will display a shortcut menu of related options for further selection.

A mouse can also be used to move items on the screen. This is achieved by first moving the mouse pointer over an item. Then, press and hold down the left mouse button and move the mouse to position the item. Finally, once you see the item in the new location, release the mouse button. This technique is called 'dragging'.

In this guide we will use the terms: Click, Double-click, Right-click and Drag to refer to mouse operations described above.

Starting Windows ME

After you switch on your computer you may be asked to log on to Windows (or to the network if your computer is linked to others). Simply type in your password and click OK.

Change your password by selecting Start menu, Settings, Control Panel.
Make sure you click on *view all Control Panel options* if they're not all displayed. Then locate and double-click on the Passwords icon.

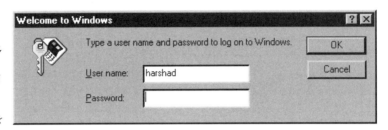

The the first time you run Windows ME the Welcome to Windows video is played on your desktop:

Once the Welcome video has stopped playing there is an overview menu of the main new features in Windows ME. Try some of these to get a basic 'feel' of the features available in Windows ME. Then click on Exit.

The Desktop

Your desktop may look different, depending on the Windows components and software you have installed, and any customisation that has been done.

If you haven't upgraded from a previous installation, your Windows ME desktop should only have a few *icons* from which all tasks can be performed easily. As a result, most of the desktop is a tidy blank area.

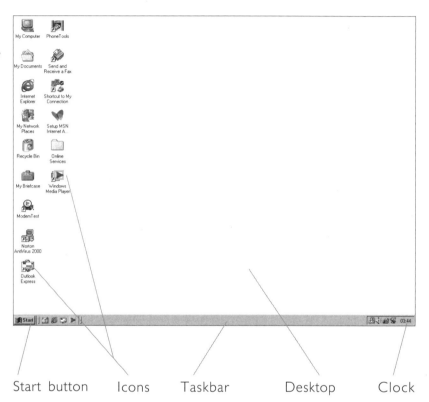

Start button   Icons   Taskbar   Desktop   Clock

Instructions in this book tell you to double-click on icons to launch the associated programs (the default).

However, you can change this to accept a single-click to open an item. See page 13 for how to switch between views.

Single-click on any icon to launch a major facility available in Windows ME – you can create your own shortcut icons for frequent programs that you'll be using.

Single-click the Start button to access and run all your programs, change settings and use the Help system.

The Taskbar at the bottom can be moved to any of the other three edges of the desktop. A Task button is created on here automatically for every program running – click on it to switch between them.

The Start Button

The Start button on the Taskbar is designed with the beginner in mind, and allows you to select and start a program quickly just with a single mouse click. Other common tasks that you need to do using your computer are also available directly from the Start button.

You can also start programs by double-clicking on desktop icons.

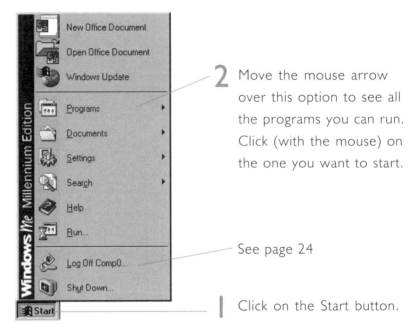

New Office Document
Open Office Document
Windows Update
Programs
Documents
Settings
Search
Help
Run...
Log Off Comp0...
Shut Down...

2 Move the mouse arrow over this option to see all the programs you can run. Click (with the mouse) on the one you want to start.

See Chapter 13, Downloading Internet Updates, for how to use Windows Update.

See page 24

Click on the Start button.

The Start button options also include:

Windows Update	Updates system files automatically
Documents	Lets you open one of the 15 most recent documents you've been working on. Also accesses My Documents and My Pictures folders
Settings	Lets you change computer settings
Search	A sophisticated search facility
Help	A complete online Help system
Run	Used to start a program
Shut Down	A safe way to switch off your computer

Switching Views

You can set Windows ME to view folders as Web pages and accept single mouse clicks to open folders.

Instead of steps 1-3 you can double-click on the Folder Options icon in the Control Panel.

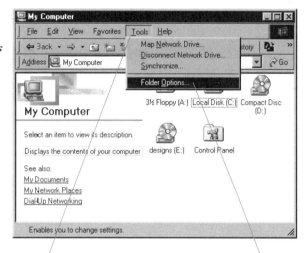

1 Double-click on My Computer icon from the desktop.

2 Click on the Tools menu.

3 Click on Folder Options...

4 Click here to have any web pages display on your desktop.

You can combine different options to create a Windows environment you prefer.

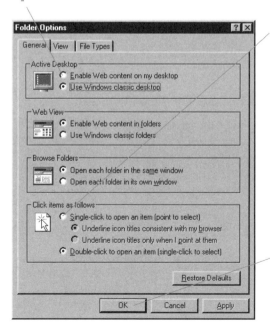

5 Click here to open a folder/window/program by single-clicking rather than the default double-click.

6 Click OK to saves the changes made.

Online Help

Right-clicking on many options, buttons and areas of Windows ME screens will display a short menu labelled 'What's This?'. Click on this to display a short explanation or definition of the item on the screen.

Click anywhere to close the explanation box.

The Windows ME Help system has been completely redesigned and improved. Choose <u>H</u>elp from the Start button, or <u>H</u>elp Topics from the <u>H</u>elp menu on some of the windows, or just press the F1 key.

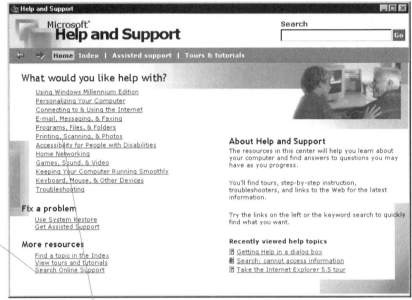

Click on Search Online Support to access the Internet and use Microsoft's online technical support site. Also see page 20.

| Click on any topic you want help on.

Printing, Scanning, & Photos

Working with printers
Copying & scanning files
Working with cameras
Working with scanners
Working with photos & graphics
Troubleshooting for printers, scanning & photos

2 Continue clicking on the links until you get to the exact help topic you're looking for.

5 Click here to get a printout of the Help topic.

6 Click here to display the Help topic in it's own full-screen window.

Use the Back and Forward buttons (like in your Internet browser) to move around the help pages.

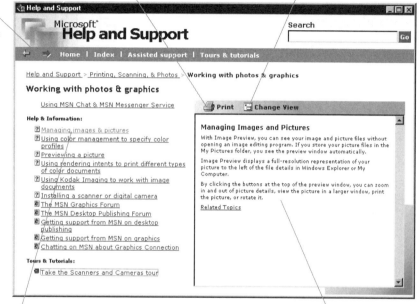

Topics prefixed with the Explorer icon connect to the Internet to provide the help.

3 Click on the appropriate topic. The ones prefixed with Question mark icons contain actual help information.

4 The Help information is displayed in the right window pane.

7 Click on the Close (X) button when you have finished.

Using the Help Index

To find specific help on how to do something in Windows Me use the Index. All topics are listed in alphabetical order here so you can find related ones easily by scrolling.

If you don't find the word you're looking for in the Index, type it in the Search box (top right) and click on Go. Windows ME will then look at all the topics that contain your word.

1 Click on the Start button and then select Help.

2 Click on the Index tab.

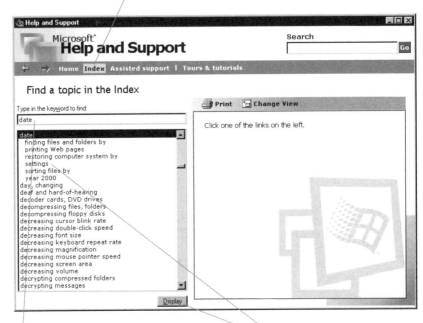

3 Type in the key letters of the word(s) you want help on. The index will automatically scroll to the start of the topics beginning with the text you typed.

4 Click on the appropriate matching phrase and then the Display button (or just double-click the phrase to save time).

...cont'd

Sometimes, Step 5 is not required: the desired topic appears immediately.

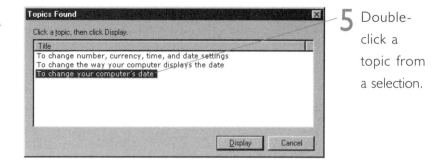

5 Double-click a topic from a selection.

6 The desired help topic appears in the right window pane.

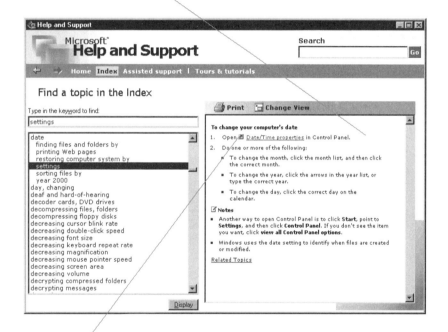

7 Click on the shortcut icon (or the related underlined text) to display the actual referenced window. For example, if you're getting help on how to change your computer's date, you can change it there and then as you are reading about it.

8 Click on the Close (X) button when you have finished.

Troubleshooters

Windows ME has an additional HELP feature: troubleshooters. Troubleshooters help you diagnose and fix technical problems.

1 Choose <u>H</u>elp from the Start button.

2 Type 'troubleshooting' in the Search box and click on Go.

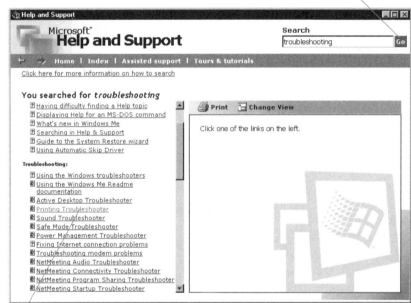

Software and hardware topics covered by troubleshooters include:

- *memory*
- *printing*
- *display*
- *sound*
- *modems*
- *home networking*
- *Internet connection*

3 Click on the appropriate link.

4 The troubleshooting diagnosis and help starts on the right pane. Follow steps 5–8 on the facing page.

Consider clicking on this icon:
to hide the Index section of the Help window (this makes it easier to work with the selected troubleshooter).

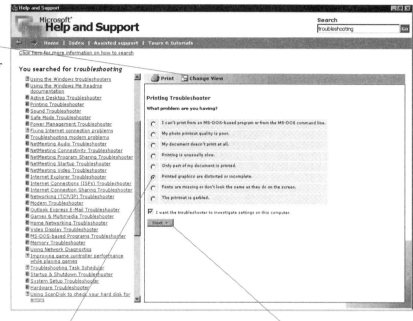

Ensure you complete the instructions in the right pane window accurately.

5 Click on a problem that applies.

6 Click on Next.

7 Complete any additional windows that are launched, as appropriate.

8 When you've finished using one or more troubleshooters, click on the Close (X) button.

Support Automation

It's likely that other people have experienced exactly the same technical problems you may be having.

Support Automation is a new facility allowing hardware and software vendors to upload to the Internet a list of problems their customers have had using their products and the solutions or workarounds to them.

You can access the relevant pages to help yourself provided you have access to the Internet.

1 Choose Help from the Start button.

2 Click on Assisted support.

You can submit technical queries directly to Microsoft, from here.
If you'd like to see new features implemented in the next version of Windows or in any other Microsoft product, just send an email to mswish@microsoft.com.

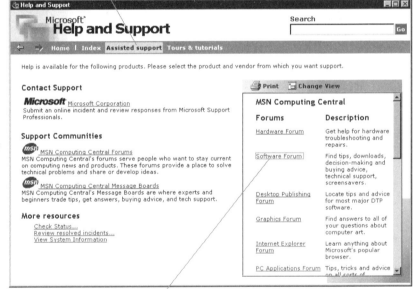

3 Click on the relevant link (if appropriate).

4 You're connected to the Internet.

Remember to close your Internet connection when you've finished.

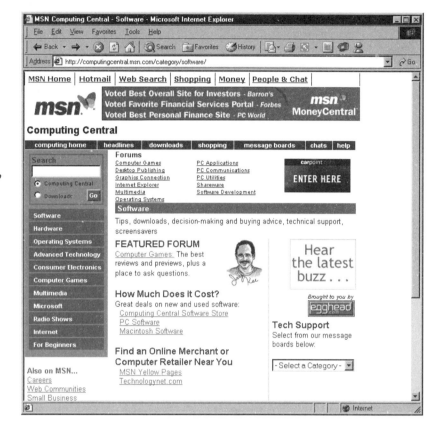

5 Follow the online links as appropriate to find the Help you need.

Wizards

Wizards can be used to install other devices, like a modem or fax, or to install a new application. Even the Installation of Windows ME itself is made easy with the help of a Wizard.

If you've been using Microsoft Word or Microsoft Excel, or even the previous version of Windows, you'll be familiar with Wizards. These guide you through a series of questions and enable you to complete a task easily. The best way to illustrate the way Wizards work is with an example. Assume that you wanted to install a printer to work with your computer:

1 Select Printers either from the Settings option available from the Start button, or from the Control Panel window.

2 Double-click on the Add Printer icon to install a new printer.

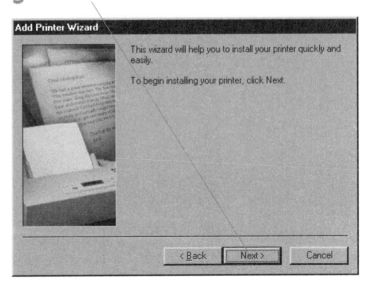

3 Click Next and follow the instructions in a series of boxes.

Windows ME uses other wizards e.g. Home Networking Wizard (Chapter 9).

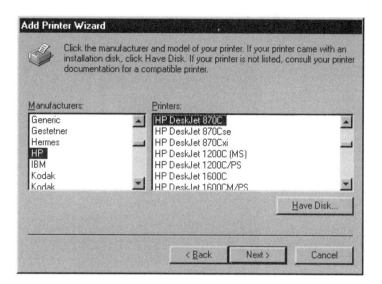

 These are further dialogs in the Add Printer Wizard...

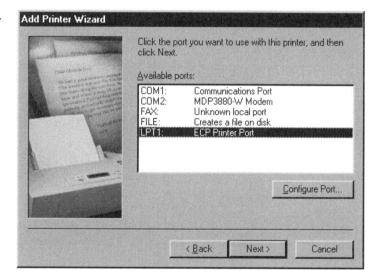

4 Click on the Back button to change options from the previous box, or Cancel to abandon the procedure altogether. Otherwise, continue to complete the dialogs, selecting Next until the last box which replaces this button with Finish. Then click on Finish.

Shutting Down your Computer and Windows ME

If your PC has been set up for multiple users (see Chapter 10), you may wish to 'log off' (rather than close down your machine) so another user can use it.
   Click here: instead of performing Step 1 follow the on-screen instructions.

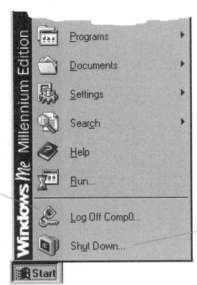

Click on the Start button, and then on Shut Down...

If you switch off your computer without following the steps here you could corrupt important files and lose valuable information.

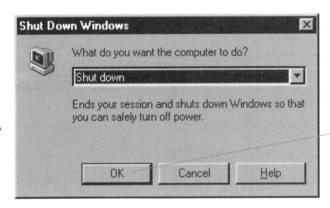

2 Click on OK.

Press Ctrl+Alt+Del keys once to close an application that has locked and twice to Restart your computer.

Normally you'll select the "Shut down" option from the drop-down menu. There is also a "Restart" option which is useful if your computer freezes or you've made changes to the system and you need these to take effect. The "Stand by" option is to conserve power. It turns off your monitor and hard disks but keeps all the programs currently running in memory open. See Configuring Power Options in Chapter 13 for further details.

Basic Controls

Everything you do in Windows ME will be done using a menu, dialog box or a window. This chapter shows you how you can use these structures.

Covers

Chapter Two

Menus

Most of the windows will have a Menu bar near the top, displaying the menu options relevant to a particular window. Simply click on a menu option to reveal a drop-down list of further options within it. As an example, we will look at the View menu from the Local Disk folder window:

A tick shows that an option is active.

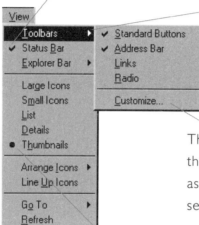

A forward arrow indicates that there is another linked menu for selection. Move the mouse arrow onto the option to see it.

The ellipse (i.e. ...) indicates that if this option is selected, an associated window with further selections will be displayed.

A bullet shows an option to be active but only one option can be selected from a group. Clicking another option from the group will automatically turn off the previously selected one.

Some examples of shortcut keys are:

Ctrl+C — COPY

Ctrl+X — CUT

Ctrl+V — PASTE

See page 52 for more information on these commands.

To deactivate an option with a tick next to it, click on it. Click on it again to activate it.

If an option is dimmed out, it cannot be used at that particular time or is not appropriate.

Some options may have shortcut keys next to them so you can use these instead of clicking on them with your mouse.

Dialog boxes

Although simple settings can be made quickly from menu options, other settings need to be made from windows displayed specifically for this purpose. These are called dialog boxes.

Tabs

Click on the appropriate one to display its settings.

Check boxes

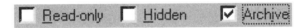

Click on as many as required. A tick indicates that the option is active. If you click on it again it will be turned off. If an option is dimmed out, it cannot be selected.

Radio buttons

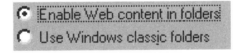

Only one out of a group of radio buttons can be selected. If you click on another radio button, the previously selected one is automatically turned off.

Action buttons

OK will save the settings selected and close the dialog box or window. Cancel will close the window without saving the amended settings – click on it if you've made a mistake. Apply will save the settings selected so far but will not close the window, in case you want to make further changes.

Structure of a window

 Dialog boxes are usually fixed-size windows and therefore don't have scroll bars, minimise, maximise, restore buttons or the control icon. They also don't display resize pointers at the edges.

All windows are similar in their structure. You can have a window containing icons for further selection, or a window that displays a screen from a program.

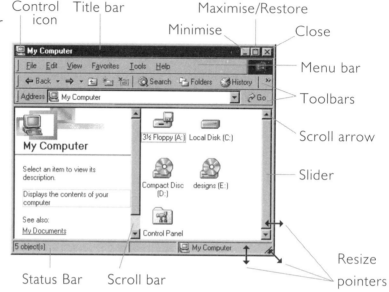

Control icon • Title bar • Minimise • Maximise/Restore • Close • Menu bar • Toolbars • Scroll arrow • Slider • Status Bar • Scroll bar • Resize pointers

 To hide the Status Bar, click on Status Bar from the View menu.

Double-click on an icon to open a window relating to it.

From the <u>V</u>iew menu, click on <u>T</u>oolbars and then select to display up to four possible ones under the menu bar.

The Status Bar displays information about items selected from the window.

The scroll bars will only appear when (as here) there are items that cannot fit into the current size of the window.

If you move the mouse pointer over any edge of a window, the pointer changes shape and becomes a double-headed resize pointer – drag it to change the size of a window. (See page 32 – Resizing a window).

Moving a window

As long as a window is not maximised, occupying the whole screen, you can move it. This is especially useful if you have several windows open and need to organise your desktop.

You can have Windows ME move the whole window as you drag the mouse, instead of just the frame.

Right-click on the desktop and click on Properties from the shortcut menu displayed. This will bring up the Display Properties dialog box – click on the Effects tab. Ensure 'Show window contents while dragging' is selected.

Finally, click on OK.

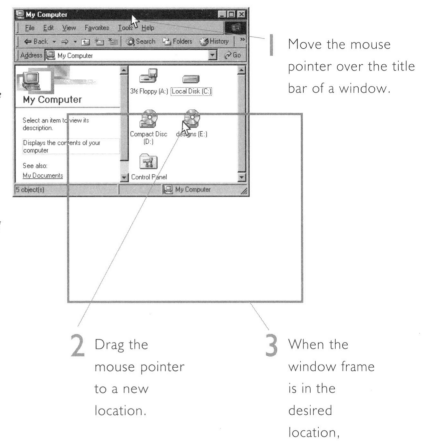

1 Move the mouse pointer over the title bar of a window.

2 Drag the mouse pointer to a new location.

3 When the window frame is in the desired location, release the mouse button.

Maximising, Minimising and Restoring a window

A window can be maximised to fill the whole screen, minimised to a button on the Taskbar, or restored to the original size.

You can also double-click on the Title bar to maximise the window.

Maximised window   Minimise button   Restore button

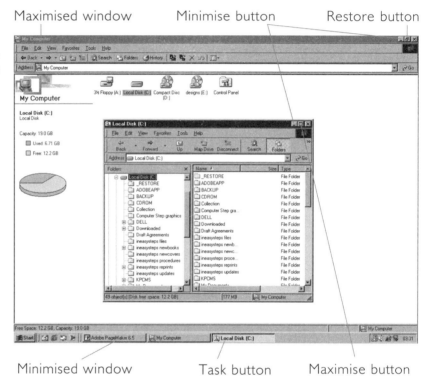

Minimised window   Task button   Maximise button

Click the Control icon (top left) or right-click the Task button, to display a shortcut menu that also allows you to minimise, maximise and restore the window.

Whether a window is maximised or original size, click on the minimise button (left of the top-right three buttons) to reduce the window to only a Task button on the Taskbar. This will create space on the desktop for you to work on other windows. When you want to restore the reduced window, simply click on it from the Taskbar.

The middle button (out of the three) can either be a maximise button, or – if the window is already maximised – the same button changes to a restore button.

Switching between windows

Switching between windows cannot be easier. The task (window) that is active always has its Title bar highlighted. If you have more than one window displayed on the desktop, click anywhere inside a window that is not active to activate it or switch to it.

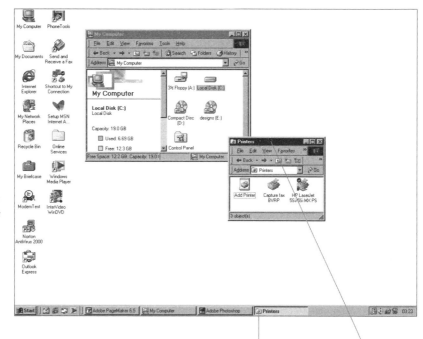

If you have too many windows open, Task buttons will resize themselves automatically.

active task button   active window

Press the Alt+Tab keys to toggle and switch between tasks.

Another method of 'task switching' is to use the Taskbar at the bottom. Every window that is open has a button created automatically on the Taskbar. Therefore, it does not matter if the window you want to switch to is overlaid with others and you cannot see it. Just click on the button for it in the Taskbar and the window will appear on top and it will be active.

Resizing a window

As long as a window is not maximised or minimised, it can be resized.

Resize and move windows on your desktop to the way you prefer to work.

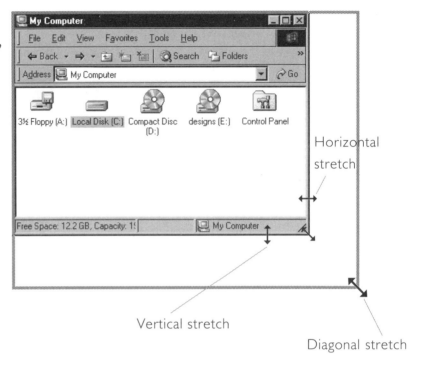

Horizontal stretch

Vertical stretch

Diagonal stretch

You can have Windows ME resize the whole window as you drag the mouse, instead of just the frame.

Click on the Start button. In the menu, click on Settings, Control Panel. In the Control Panel, select Display. Click on the Effects tab. Ensure 'Show window contents while dragging' is selected.

Finally, click OK.

1 Place the mouse arrow anywhere on the edge of a window (including corners) – it will change to a double-headed resize pointer.

2 Drag the pointer outwards to increase the size of the window, or inwards to reduce the size.

3 When the outline is in the correct position, release the mouse button – the window will now occupy the area previously shown by the outline.

Arranging windows

If you have several windows open on your desktop and want to automatically rearrange them neatly, rather than resize and move each one individually, use the Cascade or Tile options.

To avoid cluttering your desktop, try not to use the Cascade and Tile options – it is better to use the Minimize All Windows option.

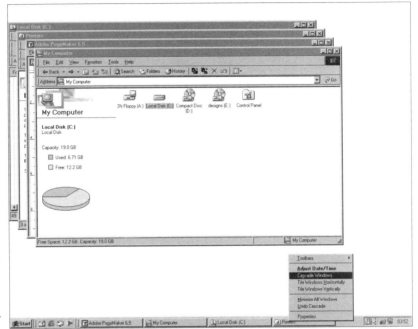

Click on Undo... (where the dots represent the original command) to restore your windows to how they were before you rearranged them.

1 Right-click on the Taskbar to display a shortcut menu.

2 Click on Cascade Windows (overlaps all the windows so that just the Title bars are visible, except for the front one), Tile Windows Horizontally (resizes each window equally and displays them across the screen in rows), or Tile Windows Vertically (resizes each window equally and displays them across the screen in columns).

Arranging icons

If you have icons displayed (large or small) in a window, you can rearrange the order, either manually or automatically.

Manually

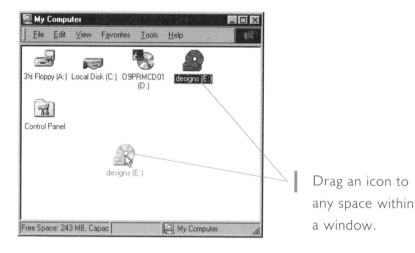

Drag an icon to any space within a window.

Automatically

You can drag an icon out of the window and onto the desktop or another window.

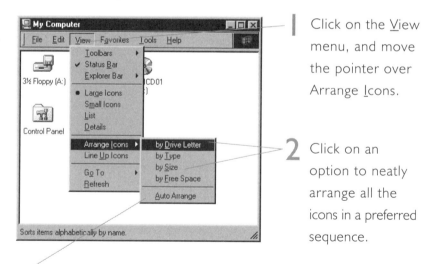

Click on the <u>V</u>iew menu, and move the pointer over Arrange <u>I</u>cons.

Click on an option to neatly arrange all the icons in a preferred sequence.

Click on <u>A</u>uto Arrange to activate it with a tick, so that if you resize the window, the icons are rearranged automatically.

Scrolling

If a window is not big enough to display all the information within it, then Scroll bars will appear automatically – either vertical, horizontal, or both. Use these to see the contents of a window not immediately in view.

The size of the Slider in relation to the Scroll bar indicates how much of the total contents are in view. The position tells you which portion is in view.

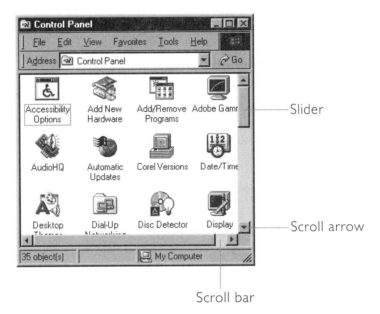

Slider

Scroll arrow

Scroll bar

| | Drag the Slider along the Scroll bar towards one of the two Scroll arrows to scroll in that direction. |

or

2 Click on the Scroll bar to scroll just a little towards the Scroll arrow nearest to it.

or

3 Click on one of the Scroll arrows to scroll just a little in that direction. Hold down your mouse button to scroll continuously.

Closing a window

When you've finished with a window you will need to close it. There are many ways of doing this – use the method you find the easiest.

Save your work before closing any program window in which you've been working.

Click on the Close button (top right corner).

If Minimised

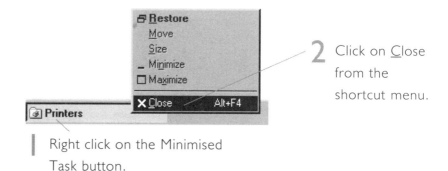

2 Click on Close from the shortcut menu.

Right click on the Minimised Task button.

From the Control icon

Click on the Control icon (top left corner).

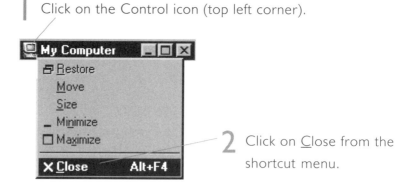

2 Click on Close from the shortcut menu.

From the keyboard

Press Alt+F4 to close the active window.

Working with Programs

Most of the time you'll be using your computer to run a program or an application you have installed. Find out how to start programs and how Windows ME can help you organise them for fast, easy access.

Covers

Chapter Three

Starting and Closing your Programs

The Start button enables you to quickly start any program listed under the Programs menu. You can add new programs to this list, or remove entries for programs not used very frequently (shown later in this chapter).

Click on the chevron to see the full list (see the second HOP TIP)

If you are using a program frequently, drag its icon onto the Start button and it will appear at the top of the Start menu for an even quicker start to that program.

To avoid a clutter, initially the Programs menu will only display the most recently used items. It assumes that you are likely to want to start one of these. If however the Program you want to start isn't there, then either wait a few seconds or click on the chevron at the bottom of the menu to expand to the full menu.

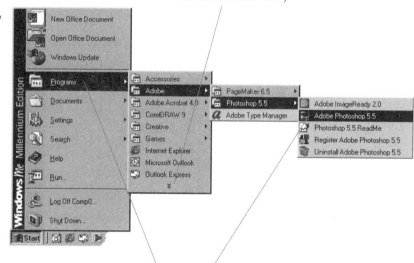

1 Click on Start and move the mouse pointer over Programs.

2 Click on a Program name you want to start. A name with a forward-arrow is a program group rather than an actual program. Move the pointer over it to display a cascaded menu of programs that are under it.

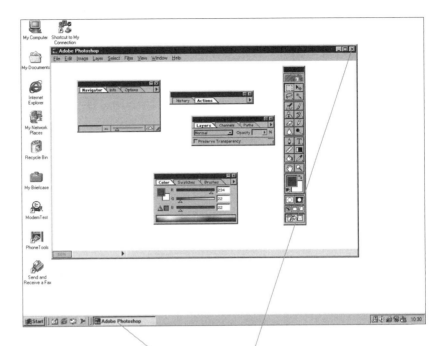

3 A button for the program appears on the Taskbar and the program starts in its own window.

4 Click on the Close button (or click on E**x**it under the **F**ile menu) to quit the program.

Starting a Program using Run

Your CD-ROM drive may have had a different letter assigned to it.

Windows ME has a special 'Run' command which is usually used to run the setup program to install a new program, from say the A: floppy disk drive or the D: CD-ROM drive. However, you can use the Run command to start any other program already installed in your computer.

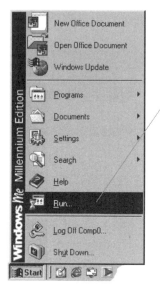

Click on the Run... option available from the Start button.

Click on the pull-down arrow to see previous commands used. Then click on one of these commands (if appropriate) instead of typing it in.

2 Type in the full name of the program, including drive and path.

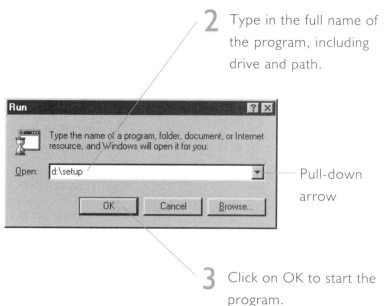

Pull-down arrow

Browse... allows you to find the program and insert the path and name in the Open box.

3 Click on OK to start the program.

Creating a Shortcut

A *Shortcut* can provide easy access to a program you use very frequently. You can place a shortcut on the desktop or in a folder.

Shortcuts can also be created to access other objects, including documents, folders, disk drives, printers, modems, faxes and even other computers.

Follow steps 1-3 to add a shortcut to a folder. However, note that Windows will not let you create shortcuts in certain pre-supplied folders e.g. My Computer, Printers and Control Panel.

If you delete a shortcut, the file that it relates to is not deleted and if you delete the file, the shortcut is not automatically deleted.

1 Drag an item onto the desktop using your right mouse button.

2 Release the mouse button to display a small menu next to the item.

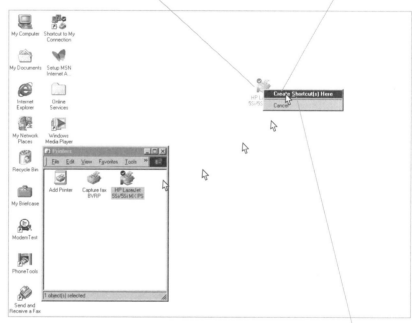

3 Click on the Create Shortcut(s) Here option. The shortcut will then appear. Note that the icon is different from the original because it has a small shortcut-arrow at the base.

Shortcut to HP LaserJet 5Si-5Si MX PS

Adding Start Menu Programs

The Programs menu displayed from the Start button can be changed to enter new programs or delete old entries that are no longer required. Changes you make here do not affect the actual programs stored on disk – these entries just allow you to start the programs quickly!

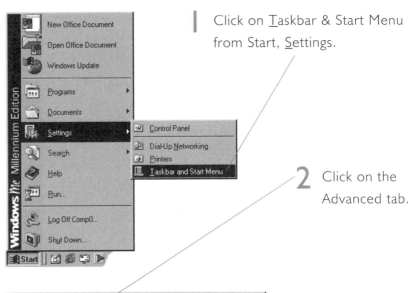

1 Click on Taskbar & Start Menu from Start, Settings.

2 Click on the Advanced tab.

Click on the Remove... button instead of the Add... button to delete an entry from the Start Programs menu.

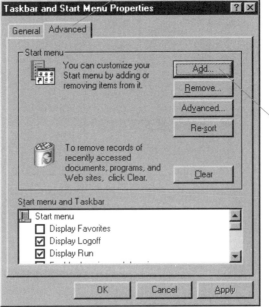

3 Click on the Add... button.

...cont'd

Click on the Browse... button if you don't know where the program is stored.

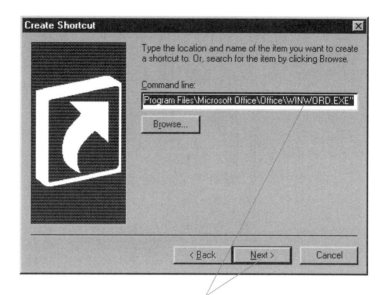

4 Type in the full name and path of the program in the Command line box and click on the Next> button.

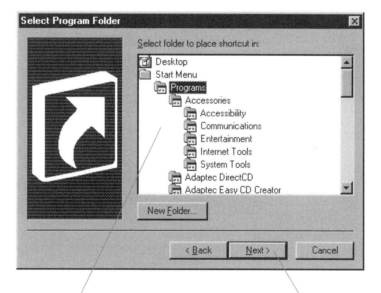

5 Select the Start Menu folder in which you want the program shortcut inserted. Click on Next.

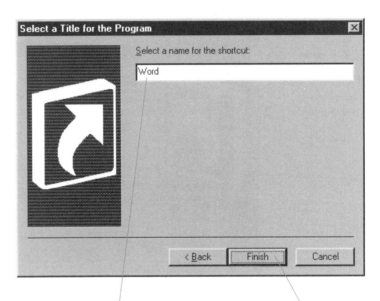

6 Type in a meaningful name for the program as you want it to appear on the Start Programs menu. Click on Finish.

7 Click on OK.

Reorganising Start Menu Items

You can move program entries, folders and shortcuts to a new location within the Start menu.

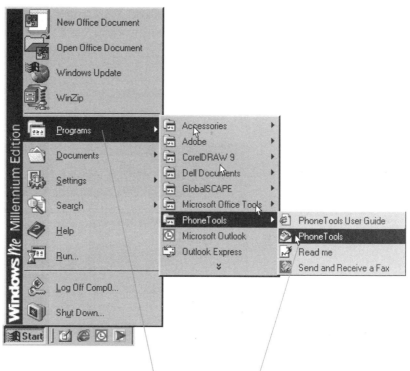

You can drag a Program entry onto the Desktop (or another window) to create a shortcut for that program there.

1 Click on Start and move the mouse pointer over the Programs option.

2 Move the mouse pointer over a program, shortcut or folder you want to move. Drag it to a new location.

Using the Startup Folder

As with the previous version of Windows, the Startup feature is available in Windows ME. This allows a program or several programs to start automatically after the computer is switched on and Windows has started. Therefore, you can start work straight away on a program that you always use.

A shortcut to starting Windows Explorer is by right-clicking on the Start button and selecting Explore from the short menu.

| Click on Windows Explorer available from the Start button, Programs, Accessories.

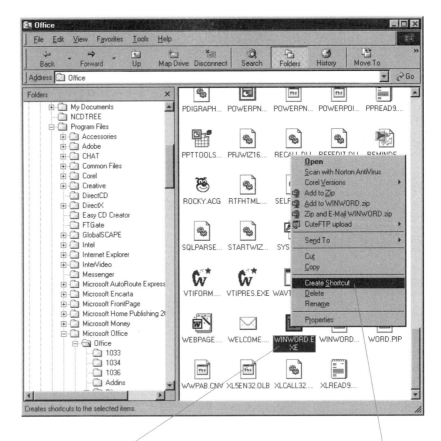

2 Find the program you want and right-click on it.

3 From the small menu displayed, click on Create Shortcut. A shortcut icon of the program selected is created.

...cont'd

 You can use this technique to move any program to any folder.

 To display the StartUp folder may need to click on the plus sign next to the Windows folder to expand the hierarchy of folders under it, then on the Start Menu entry, and then on the Programs folder. The StartUp folder should be in this last Programs folder.

4 From the left column of folders, find the StartUp folder. The path is C:\WINDOWS\Start Menu\Programs\StartUp.

5 Drag the shortcut icon created onto the Startup folder. The program it relates to will now start automatically each time you start Windows.

Starting Programs Minimised

Sometimes you may want to start a program but not have it take over most of the desktop. You therefore need to set it up so that when it's started it is minimised automatically. When you are ready to use the program you will then only need to click on its button on the Taskbar.

1 Click on the Start button with your right mouse button and click on <u>O</u>pen from the shortcut menu displayed.

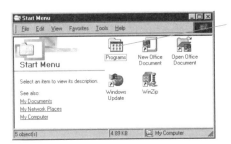

2 Double-click on the Programs folder.

3 Double-click on the StartUp folder.

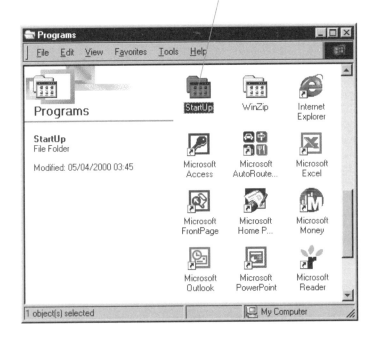

...cont'd

4 Right-click on a program you want to start Minimised. Then select Properties from the shortcut menu.

As an alternative to step 4 you can first select the Program item and then click on File and then Properties from the menu bar.

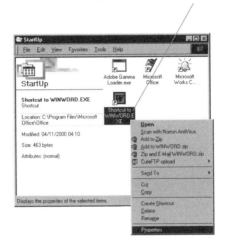

You may want several programs to start automatically when Windows starts. It is best to have them minimised, as in this example, so you can easily access them as you need to from the Taskbar.

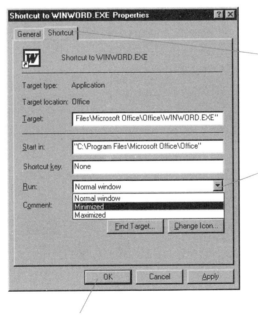

5 Click on the Shortcut tab.

6 Click on Minimized after clicking on the pull-down arrow.

7 Click on OK.

Install and Uninstall Programs

You can add (Install) new programs or just the uninstalled components of an existing program. You can also remove (Uninstall) a program – this feature is similar to that provided by the special Uninstaller utilities on the market. Note that Windows ME can only uninstall programs specifically developed to use this feature.

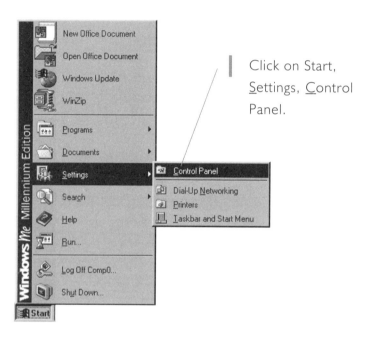

Click on Start, Settings, <u>C</u>ontrol Panel.

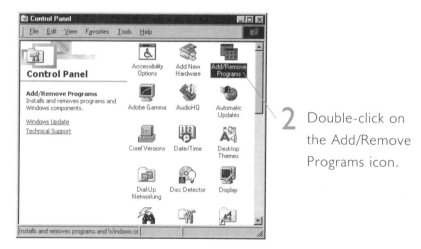

2 Double-click on the Add/Remove Programs icon.

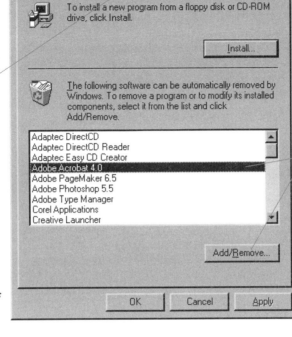

3 Make sure the Install/ Uninstall tab is selected.

Use the Windows Setup tab to Add/ Remove Windows ME components.

4 Click on an application and then on the Add/ Remove... button.

Some programs require you to insert the original CD or floppy disks before you can continue.

5 Complete the further dialogs/messages which launch. Note the following:

- Some programs launch a tailor-made uninstall routine – simply follow the on-screen instructions.

- Other programs produce this message:

You may have to restart Windows when installation or uninstallation is complete.

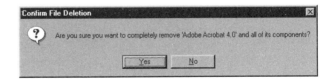

Click on Yes above and follow any further instructions.

Cut, Copy and Paste

You can move or copy information (text, graphics, etc.) from one Windows program to another, or within the same program, through a temporary storage area called the clipboard.

You can also use Cut, Copy and Paste from the Edit menu.

Press the Print Screen key on your keyboard to copy your screen display to the clipboard.

1 Start a Program, say Paint, and select an area.

2 Right-click and select Copy from the menu displayed to copy the selection to the clipboard (Cut is the same but deletes the selection, too).

If you cut or copy another object, the previous one will be lost. Switching off has the same effect.

You can save the contents of the clipboard by choosing Start, Programs, Accessories, System Tools, Clipboard Viewer.

3 Start another program, say WordPad.

4 Right-click and select Paste to insert the clipboard contents.

Saving your Work

Whichever program you work with, at some stage you will need to save your work (letter, spreadsheet, drawing, etc.) as a file. There are two types of saves: changes to an existing file (Save), and saving a new file created for the first time (Save As).

Just click on Save to save the changes to an existing named file.

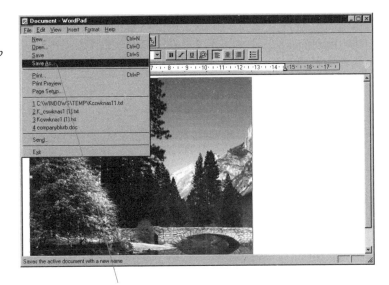

| From the File menu, click on Save As...

Use Save As to copy a file by giving it another name/ location.

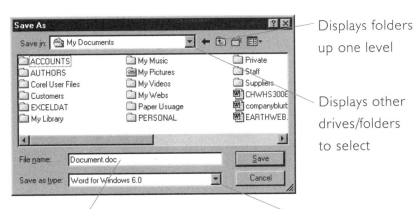

Displays folders up one level

Displays other drives/folders to select

2 Type in a name here for your new file and click on the Save button.

Displays other file types you can save in

The MS-DOS Prompt

Unlike previous versions of Windows, Windows ME doesn't rely on the older MS-DOS system. It has been re-written to take out the MS-DOS dependency completely, making it faster and more efficient. However, if you still like to use MS-DOS commands, there is an MS-DOS simulator.

From the Start button, select Programs, Accessories, MS-DOS Prompt. The MS-DOS Prompt window displayed is like any other window, including title bar, control buttons (minimise, maximise, close), scroll bars, resize capability. A button is even inserted on the Taskbar. You can type any MS-DOS command at the prompt.

Press Alt+Enter to make the MS-DOS Prompt window full-screen if it is windowed, or vice versa.

Font/size   Mark   Copy   Paste   Full-screen   Close

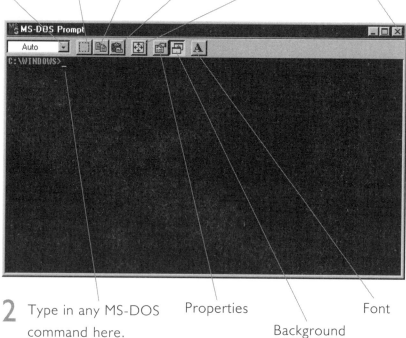

2 Type in any MS-DOS command here.   Properties   Background   Font

3 Click on the Close button (or type Exit and press Enter) to close the MS-DOS Prompt window.

Accessing Information

The means of accessing or browsing local information (on your computer) and external information (on the Internet/network) is very similar.

Covers

Chapter Four

My Computer

One way to look for all your files, regardless of where they are stored, involves using My Computer, usually located on the top left corner of the desktop.

My Computer

Double-click on this icon.

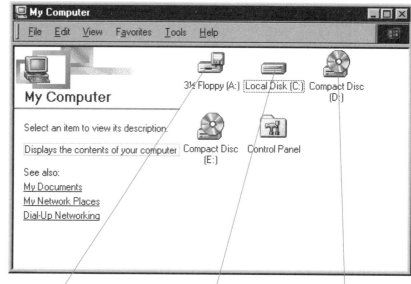

This computer has a second writable CD drive (E:) which you may not have.

Files in your 3.5" floppy disk drive

Files in your main hard disk C:

Files in your CD-ROM drive

2 Double-click on the appropriate drive icon from the My Computer window.

...cont'd

A file is a basic unit of storage. All your programs and documents are stored as files.

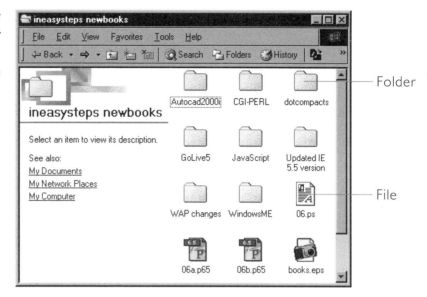

Folder

File

A Folder is the same as the older term, directory. It is used to store files.

3 Double-click on a folder to display files it contains or other folders.

To make it easy for you to identify which files belong to which applications you'll find that most file types will have their unique icons. So for example:

Word   Notepad   Internet Explorer

Excel   Media Player   Acrobat

PowerPoint   WinZip   Picture It!

Paint   PageMaker   Access

Windows Explorer

Another way to look at your files is to use Windows
Explorer.

Starting Windows Explorer

*Right-click on
the Start
button and
click on Explore
in the shortcut
menu for a faster start.*

Click on
the Start
button.

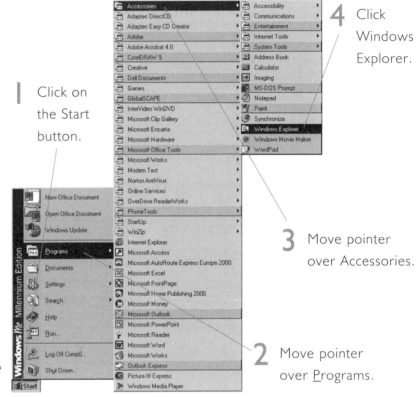

4 Click
Windows
Explorer.

3 Move pointer
over Accessories.

*Also right-click
on other icons
from the
desktop, or on
a folder, and
then click on Explore to start
Explorer showing the
contents of the item chosen.
Note, however, that this
technique does not work
with shortcut icons.*

2 Move pointer
over Programs.

Other ways of starting Windows Explorer

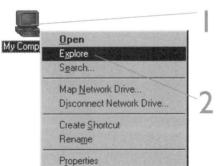

1 Right-click the My Computer
icon on the desktop.

2 Click on Explore from the
shortcut menu displayed.

...cont'd

Or:

This technique shows the contents of the selected folder in Explorer.

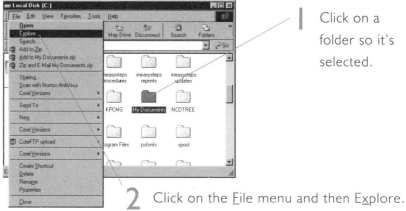

| Click on a folder so it's selected.

2 Click on the <u>F</u>ile menu and then E<u>x</u>plore.

Windows Explorer display

When you make any changes in Explorer, remember to press F5 to refresh the display.

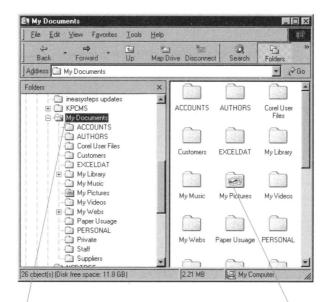

| Click on a folder you want to see the contents of. Folders and the files they contain are displayed on the right side.

2 Double-click a program icon to start it, or a document/folder icon to open it.

Both Windows Explorer and My Computer (provided you have Folders view on – View, Explorer Bar, Folders) display a structured hierarchy of all your drives and folders on the left. Click on a plus sign next to a folder to see other folders it contains, and on a minus sign to hide this detail.

Expand folder

Collapse folder

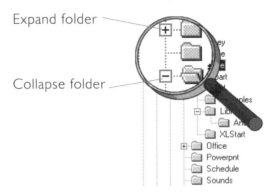

Altering the split between panes

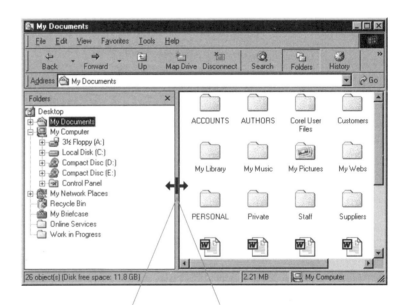

| 1 | Move the mouse pointer over the border so that it becomes double-headed. | 2 | Drag the border towards left or right, as appropriate. |

Changing the Display

Whether you are using Windows Explorer or displaying files using My Computer, you can change the display of files by using the View menu.

Click on the View menu option.

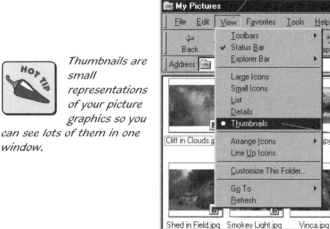

Thumbnails are small representations of your picture graphics so you can see lots of them in one window.

2 Click on one of the display options.

An example...

The Details option (from the View menu) shows the size of file, type, and when it was last modified

Sorting the Contents of a window

Windows allows you to sort your files in any drive or folder (including even the desktop) by name, type, date and size.

1 Click on the View menu option.

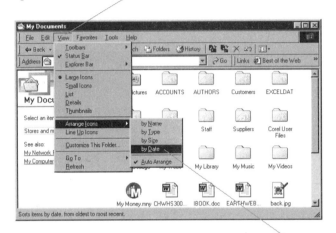

2 Click on Arrange Icons and then one of the sort by options.

It is very useful to display your files in Details view. Then you can click on any column heading to sort the list by that field, or click on it again to sort it in reverse order.

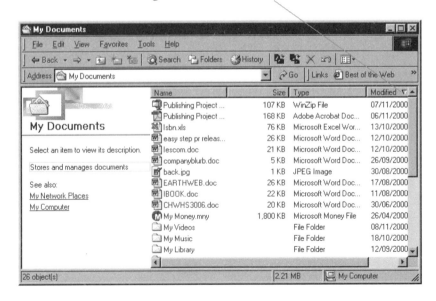

Active Desktop

In Windows ME you can turn your Desktop to display 'active content' – this is content from the web that keeps changing rather than displaying a static wallpaper or background. Examples include stock ticker (to constantly keep up-to-date with stock prices), headline news, travel and weather information, to name but a few. You can add items from the Active Desktop Gallery, your favourite web sites/channels or even your own web site.

Shortcut: Right-click a link in any web page and drag it to your desktop. Then click 'Create Active Desktop item(s) Here'.

1 Right-click on the Desktop and move your mouse pointer on Active Desktop. Then select Customise My Desktop.

2 From the Web tab ensure that 'Show Web content on my Active Desktop' is ticked.

3 Click on the New... button. If you want to download an item from Microsoft's Active Desktop Gallery, click the Visit Gallery button to go onto the Internet. Alternatively, if you want to add from any other web site, type its Web address in the Location box.

The Standard Buttons Toolbar

Launching

Windows ME provides four toolbars:

- *Standard Buttons*
- *Address Bar*
- *Links*
- *Radio*

found in Windows Explorer, My Computer and other folders.

There are other toolbars, displayed on the Taskbar – see page 68.

Click on View, Toolbars, Standard Buttons so that it is activated and ticked.

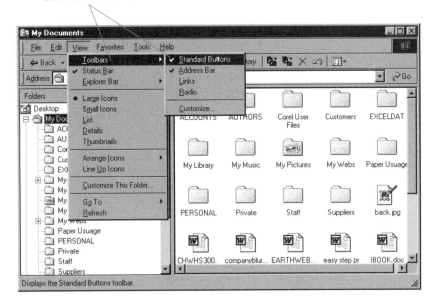

Using

Shortcut key: Press Backspace to see the higher level folder/drive.

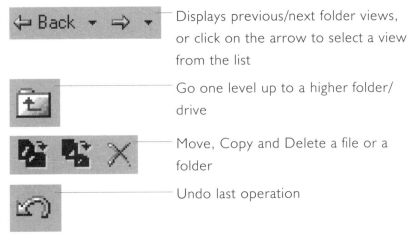

Displays previous/next folder views, or click on the arrow to select a view from the list

Go one level up to a higher folder/drive

Move, Copy and Delete a file or a folder

Undo last operation

Views – change the display of files/folders (same as from the View menu)

The Standard toolbar buttons are automatically replaced by Internet browser ones if you access the Internet. See page 102.

The Address Toolbar

Launching

The Address Bar allows you to select and display contents from the main drives and folders in your system as well as from the Internet.

I Click on View, Toolbars, Address Bar so that it is activated and ticked.

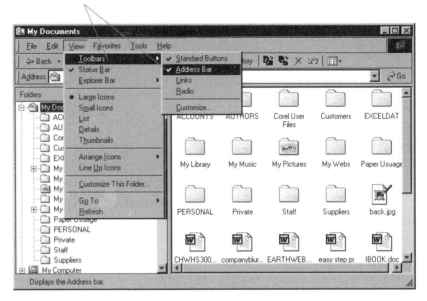

Using

You can type in any Internet web address here (or URL) to access it. Then press the Enter key. See also page 100.

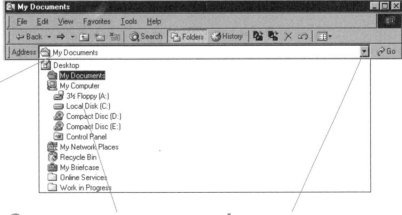

2 Click on a drive or a folder to have its contents display.

I Click on the down-arrow.

The Links Toolbar

Launching

The Links toolbar provides shortcuts to major World Wide Web sites (you don't have to pre-load your browser). See also page 101.

Click on View, Toolbars, Links so that it is activated and ticked.

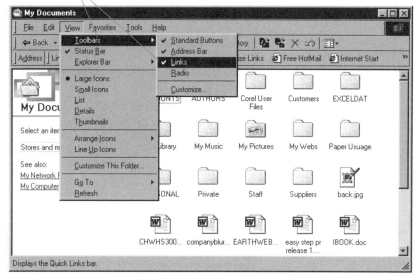

To use the Links toolbar, you must have a live Internet connection.

Using

Click on a Web address.

Switching between the Standard Buttons, Address and Links toolbars

Double-click to fully display or drag above/below/on other toolbars.

Drag vertical bar to control how much of a toolbar shows when it shares space with another.

The Radio Toolbar

Launching

The Radio toolbar (as part of Windows Media Player) allows you to listen to radio stations from around the world. See also page 101.

| Click on View, Toolbars, Radio so that it is activated and ticked.

Using

To use the Radio toolbar, you must have a live Internet connection.

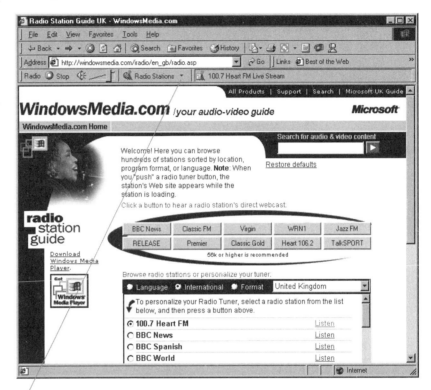

The Radio toolbar can be dragged up/down to share space with other toolbars in the same way as Address and Links toolbars.

2 Click here and select Radio Station Guide. You'll be connected to the Internet. From here you can select and listen to any radio station (make sure your speakers are on). Often the specific radio station's website window will pop up, showing the title of the track playing, artist and the album the track is from.

Displaying New Toolbars

New toolbars appear on the Taskbar. To make one visible:

There are two further preset toolbars which can only display on the Taskbar (by default) or the desktop itself:

- *Quick Launch*
- *Desktop*

Use Quick Launch to access often-used features e.g: Show Desktop, Internet Explorer Browser, Windows Media Player.
Use Desktop to access all of your shortcuts, in one convenient place.

2 Click on Toolbars. Then click on the relevant toolbar.

Quick Launch toolbar

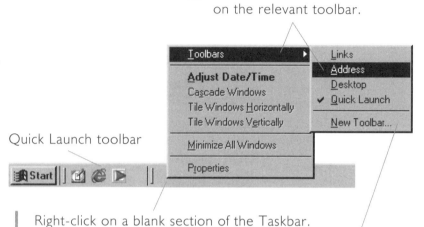

Right-click on a blank section of the Taskbar.

Click here to create your own toolbars based on the contents of any drives/folders (including web sites)

The Taskbar showing the Address toolbar

Use the techniques shown here to make the Quick Launch and Desktop toolbars visible.

The Taskbar showing the Desktop toolbar

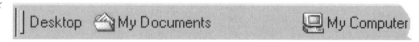

Repositioning Toolbars

You can reposition toolbars on the desktop itself:

If you want to return a toolbar to the Taskbar, simply drag it there.

2 Release the mouse button to confirm the move.

To resize/move a toolbar on the Taskbar, drag the vertical bar:

Drag here to the left or right

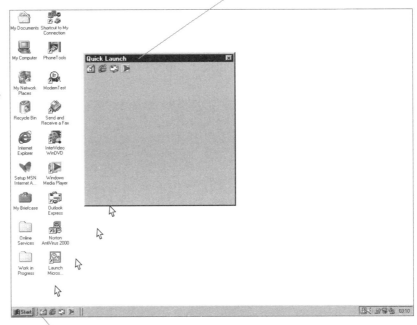

1 Drag a toolbar onto the desktop.

Use standard techniques to resize/reposition toolbars on the desktop.

In the above example, the Quick Launch toolbar is being relocated onto the desktop.

Extending the Quick Launch toolbar

You can drag any shortcuts you create on the desktop (see page 41) to the Quick Launch toolbar for fast easy access.

e.g. Windows Explorer

Browsing with Multiple windows

By default when you have one folder window displayed and you open another folder the contents of the new folder are displayed in the same window. This is fine for most uses but sometimes it's useful to have the contents of a new folder display in a new window. For example, for when you need to move or copy files between open folders.

If you open each folder in its own window, your desktop may soon be cluttered with windows you don't need.

From any folder window, click on the Tools menu and then Folder Options...

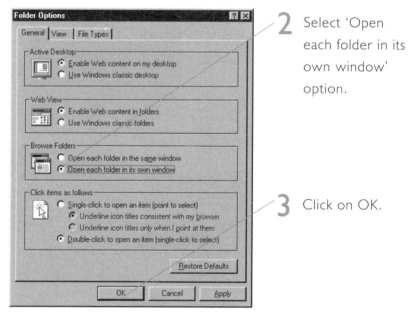

2 Select 'Open each folder in its own window' option.

3 Click on OK.

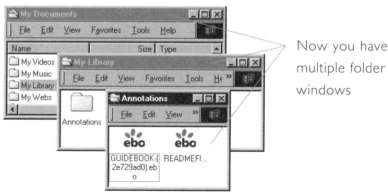

Now you have multiple folder windows

Creating a Shortcut to your Files

You can create a shortcut to any drive, folder or file as
described on page 41. You can also create a shortcut of your
entire local hard disk to the Start menu. This will provide an
easy menu system of all your folders and files like you
already have for starting Programs.

| Drag your main disk drive icon from the My Computer
folder and onto the Start button.

2 Use the cascaded menu hierarchy as shown here to access
any folder/file.

Different Ways of Opening your Files

Windows ME offers several ways of opening your files and the programs that created them without having to first start the appropriate program and then to open the file from within that program.

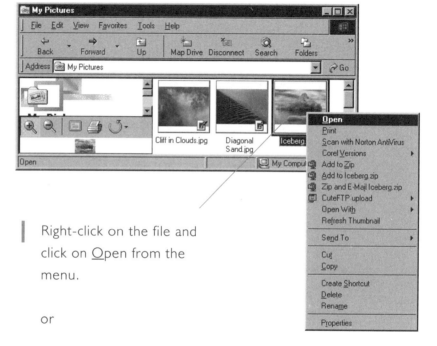

These easy techniques for opening files without first opening the application works because different file formats are already associated with particular applications.

To change an association or to create a new one select *Tools, Folder Options..., File Types* tab from any folder window.

1 Right-click on the file and click on <u>O</u>pen from the menu.

or

2 Click on the file to select it and then choose <u>O</u>pen from the <u>F</u>ile menu.

or

3 Just double-click on the file icon.

or

4 Drag the file icon onto the application icon, either on the desktop or a folder.

or

5 Drag the file icon over the Taskbar program button. When the Program window opens, drag the icon into its window; only then release the mouse button.

Recently Used Documents

Quite often you'll want to open a document you have been working on recently. Windows stores details of the latest 15 documents you've been using. Find them under the Start button, <u>D</u>ocuments for a faster access to them again.

Click here for rapid access to My Documents or My Pictures folders.

You can also access the 'My Documents' folder from the Desktop (provided 'Show My Documents on the Desktop' check box is ticked in the View tab from Folder Options dialog box via the Tools menu in a window) or from the left pane of Windows Explorer.

You can clear the display of these documents by selecting Settings, Taskbar and Start Menu, Advanced tab, and clicking on the Clear button. Finally, click on OK.

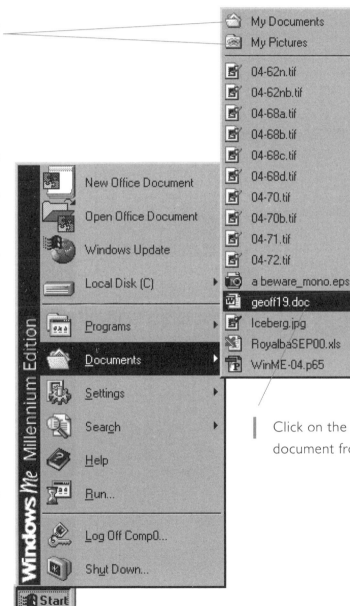

Click on the required document from this list.

File Properties

Every item – file, folder, program, shortcut, device – has Properties. You can access the Properties dialog box for all in the same way. The purpose is twofold:

- to display basic information about the item
- to change settings for the item

There are some third party programs in this shortcut menu which you may not have.

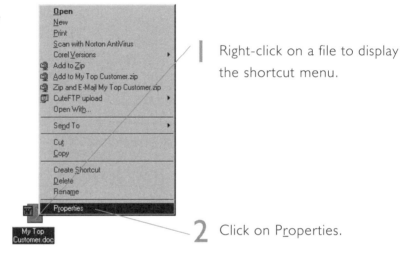

Right-click on a file to display the shortcut menu.

2 Click on Properties.

Managing Files and Folders

Remember that Folders are just logical names where files are stored. Windows handles operations on Files and Folders (like moving, copying, deleting, etc.) in a similar way and so they are both covered together here.

Covers

Chapter Five

Selecting Multiple Files/Folders

To select a single file or folder you simply click on it to highlight it. Then you can move, copy or delete it (see the next topic). However, if you want to perform these operations on several files or folders you'll need to select all of them, so that they can then be manipulated efficiently, in one fell swoop.

Adjacent block of files

To de-select all files, click once anywhere outside the selection area.

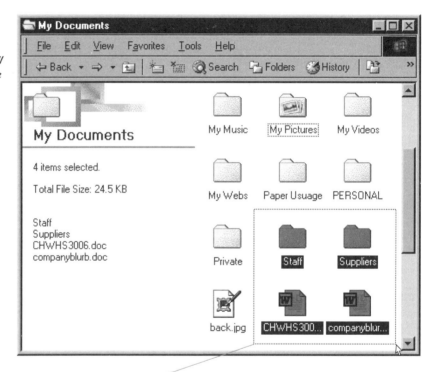

Selecting files here can include whole folders, which may contain other files.

1 Drag out a box to cover all the files you want selected.

   or

2 Click on the first item to select it. Then press and hold down the SHIFT key and click on the last item in the group to highlight the whole group, indicating that it's selected.

Non-adjacent files

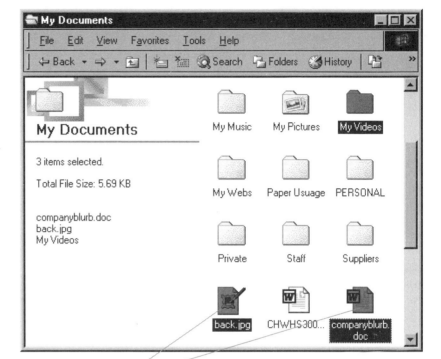

To de-select a file, Ctrl+click on it again.

| To select several non-adjacent files, press and hold down the Ctrl key. Then click on as many files as required. If they're highlighted they're selected.

Press Ctrl+A to select all files and folders in the active window.

To select all files (and folders) in a window, click on Select <u>A</u>ll from the <u>E</u>dit menu.

Copying and Moving Files/Folders

You may want to copy/move a file to the same disk (a different folder) or to another (e.g. a floppy) disk. There are several ways you can achieve this. For speed and simplicity, however, the first method – using the right mouse button – is recommended.

Using the right mouse button

Instead of a single file you can copy/move multiple files (just select as shown in the last topic), or copy/move a folder using the same technique.

1 Start Windows Explorer. In the window on the left, select the folder that contains the file you want to copy or move.

2 In the window on the right, select the file you want to copy or move.

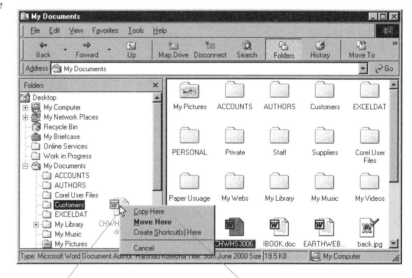

3 Using the right mouse button drag the file you want to copy/ move onto the destination folder or drive (in the window on the left) so that it is highlighted. Then release to display a shortcut menu.

4 Click on the Move Here or Copy Here option.

...cont'd

Using the left mouse button

For all these operations you can also use the My Computer display instead of Windows Explorer.

In both cases, ensure Folders view is active: View menu, Explorer Bar, Folders (or simply click on Folders from the Standard Buttons toolbar).

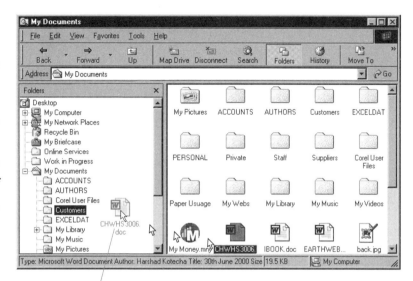

I Using the left mouse button drag a file (or multiple files/ folders) to the destination folder or drive in the window on the left.

2 To move/copy files to the same drive or to another drive, follow this simple technique:

You'll notice a little '+' symbol in a box if the file is going to be copied. Otherwise, the file will be moved.

Copy to another drive	Just drag
Move to another drive	Hold down the Shift key when dragging
Copy to same drive	Hold down the Ctrl key when dragging
Move to same drive	Just drag

Using Cut, Copy, Paste

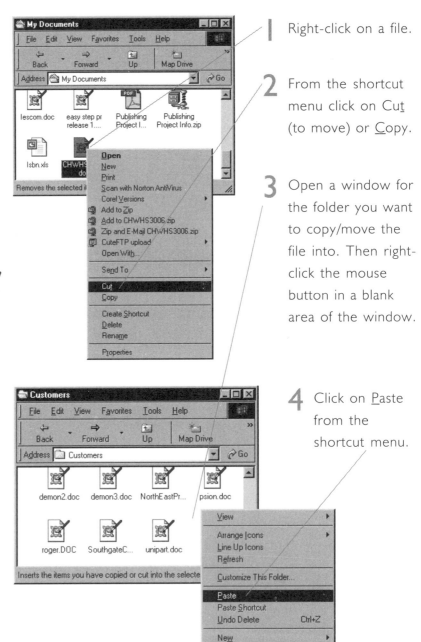

You can also use Cut, Copy and Paste from the Edit menu.

1 Right-click on a file.

2 From the shortcut menu click on Cut (to move) or Copy.

3 Open a window for the folder you want to copy/move the file into. Then right-click the mouse button in a blank area of the window.

4 Click on Paste from the shortcut menu.

...cont'd

Explicitly to a Floppy disk

Make sure there is a floppy disk in your drive before copying or moving files to it.

Use the same technique to copy/move files to another type of drive you may have. e.g. Writable CD, Removable disk.

Keep the Shift key pressed when selecting the floppy disk to Move the file instead of Copying it.

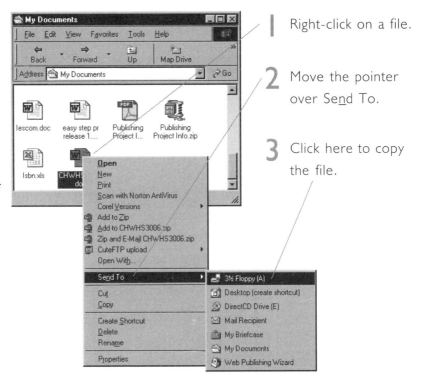

1 Right-click on a file.

2 Move the pointer over Send To.

3 Click here to copy the file.

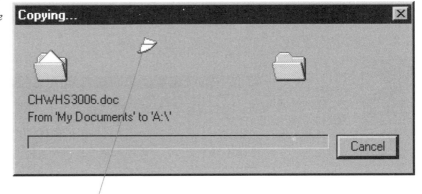

A progress bar with an animation of a file flying across is shown whenever a file (or group of files) is moved, copied or deleted.

Deleting Files/Folders

Deleting files and folders is easy and safe in Windows ME (see the next topic, Recycle Bin, too). Note that you can delete a file from wherever it is listed, although the My Computer display is shown here.

 You can press the Delete key on your keyboard instead of selecting Delete from the menu.

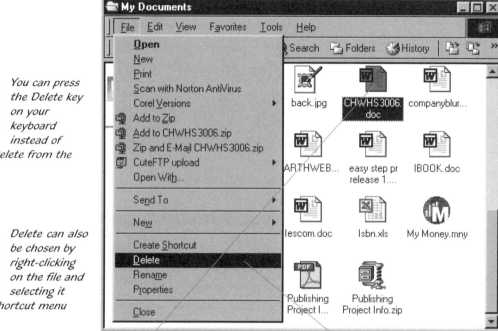

 Delete can also be chosen by right-clicking on the file and selecting it from the shortcut menu displayed.

| Select one or more files/folders (see earlier topic).

2 Click on Delete from the File menu.

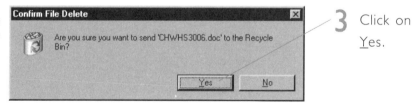

3 Click on Yes.

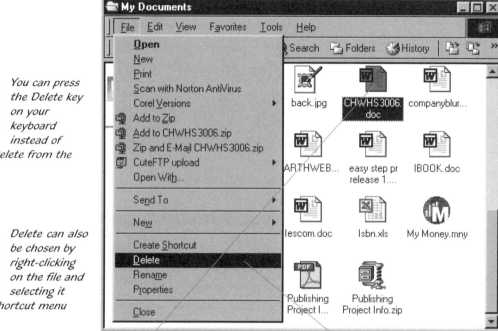 *You can also delete a file by dragging it onto the Recycle Bin icon on the desktop.*

If you suddenly realise that you have made a mistake deleting one or more files, choose Undo Delete from the Edit menu straightaway. Alternatively, use the Recycle Bin to retrieve it (see next topic).

The Recycle Bin

Files that you delete from your floppy disk or from the MS-DOS command prompt don't go into the Recycle Bin.

The Recycle Bin is a place where deleted files are kept. They are not physically deleted from your hard disk until you 'empty' the Recycle Bin (or erase them within the Bin itself). The Recycle Bin therefore provides a safety net for files you may delete by mistake and allows you to easily retrieve them.

A drawback of the Recycle Bin is that from time to time, you'll have to empty it to free up disk space taken up by deleted files.

Restoring files

Recycle Bin

Double-click on the Recycle Bin icon from the desktop.

You can also restore folders.

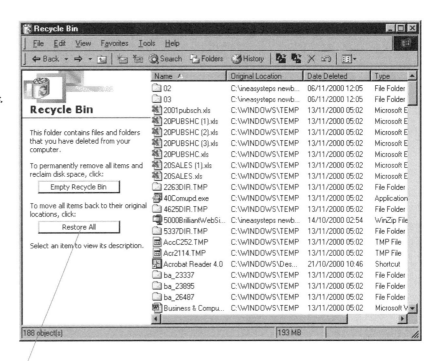

2 Click on Restore All, or select a file/multiple files (as shown on pages 76–77) and this button changes to just Restore.

Emptying the Recycle Bin

Recycle Bin

I Double-click on the Recycle Bin icon from the desktop.

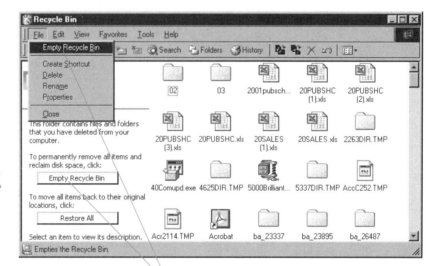

If you only want to erase certain files in the Bin, select them. Omit steps 2-3. Instead, click on Delete in the File menu. In the Confirm File Delete dialog, click on Yes.

2 Click on Empty Recycle Bin from the File menu, or from the button on the left, to reclaim lost disk space.

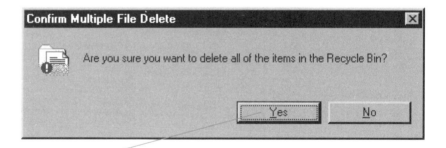

3 Click on Yes.

...cont'd

Bypassing the Recycle Bin

If you opt to bypass the Recycle Bin, you'll need to be even more careful when deleting files.

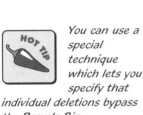

You can use a special technique which lets you specify that individual deletions bypass the Recycle Bin.

Don't follow steps 1–2. Instead, select the file/ folder(s) you want to delete, then simply hold down one SHIFT key as you press the Delete key.

Finally, in the Confirm File Delete dialog, click on Yes.

If you want, you can have Windows ME *permanently* erase files or folders when you delete them – in other words, they aren't copied to the Recycle Bin.

Right-click on the Recycle Bin icon. Then click Properties.

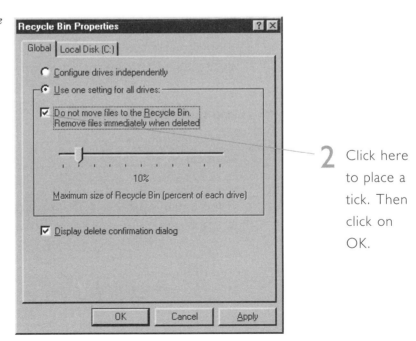

2 Click here to place a tick. Then click on OK.

Creating a New File/Folder

You can create new files in standard formats for use with specific programs installed on your computer. You can also create new folders to organise your work into.

The New option to create a file/folder is also accessible from the desktop. Just right-click the mouse button.

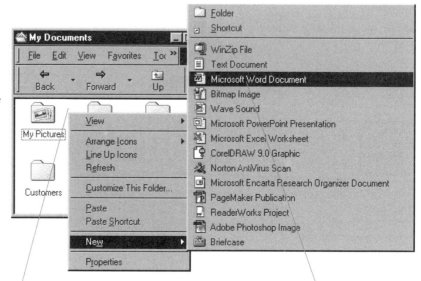

| Open a folder (from My Computer or Windows Explorer) you want to create a file or folder in and right-click on an empty part of the window.

2 Move the pointer over New, and then click on Folder to create a new folder. To create a file click on one of the file formats in the bottom section of the menu.

3 Type a name for the file/folder created and then press the ENTER key.

Renaming a File/Folder

You can rename a file/folder at any time. It is done very easily too, by simply editing the current name.

Use the same method to rename icons on the desktop. You won't be able to rename the Recycle Bin though!

1 Right-click on a file/folder. Then click on Rename in the shortcut menu.

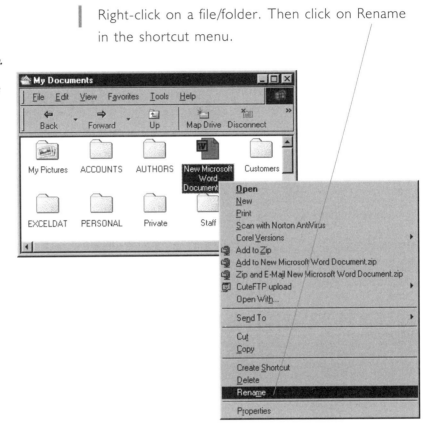

2 The current name will be boxed in heavy line. Type the new name, or use the cursor arrow keys to position the cursor and edit only part of the name.

3 Press the ENTER key or click your mouse pointer outside the file name to confirm the new name.

Backtracking File Operations

If you accidentally delete, rename, copy or move a file, you can undo (reverse) the operation. Furthermore, you can even undo several preceding operations instead of just the last one (multi-level undo feature).

Undo mistakes as soon as possible before performing other valid operations.

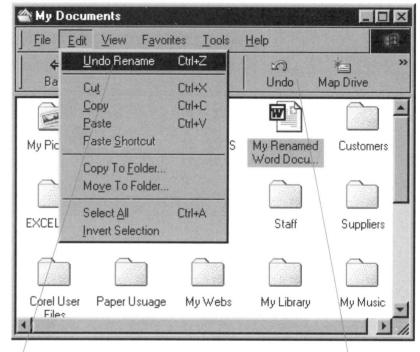

Click on the Edit menu from any folder. An Undo of the last file operation is displayed. Click on it and repeat if necessary.

or

Click on Undo from the Standard Buttons toolbar.

Searching for Files/Folders

The Search feature in Windows ME is very powerful. The search can be based on partial file names, specific dates, given file types/sizes or text within the files. Once the desired files are found you can open them or perform other operations (including deleting, renaming, copying, displaying properties, etc.) – all from the search results displayed!

For more elaborate searches, see page 90.

You can also activate the Windows ME Search feature through the Start button, Search, For Files or Folders.

Click on the Search button from any folder window.

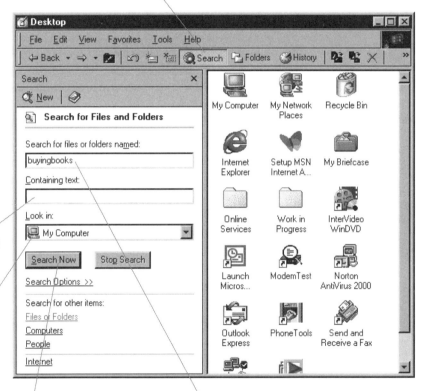

To search for text within files, type in the search text.

To limit the search to specific drives or computers, select it here.

2 Click and then type in full/part name of the file or folder.

3 Click here to start the search.

Search Options: searches by date range

To search for files within a specific date range:

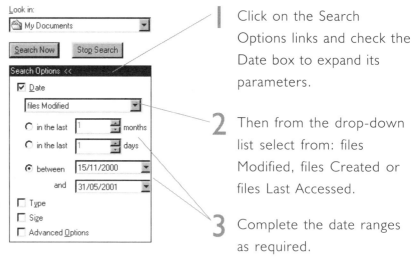

1 Click on the Search Options links and check the Date box to expand its parameters.

2 Then from the drop-down list select from: files Modified, files Created or files Last Accessed.

3 Complete the date ranges as required.

The actions described here are optional, and supplement the basic search procedures described on page 89. Carry out the steps here before you perform step 3 on page 89.

Search Options: searches by file type/size

To search for files of a specific type or size:

From the Search Options link check the Type box and then select a file type from the drop-down list.

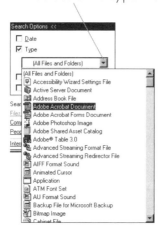

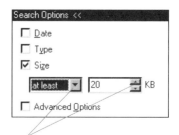

To further limit the search select 'at least' or 'at most' and a file size (in kilobytes).

Acting on search results

When a search has been completed, this is the result:

A preview and a link to the folder where the file resides appears in the top pane after you select a file from the lower pane.

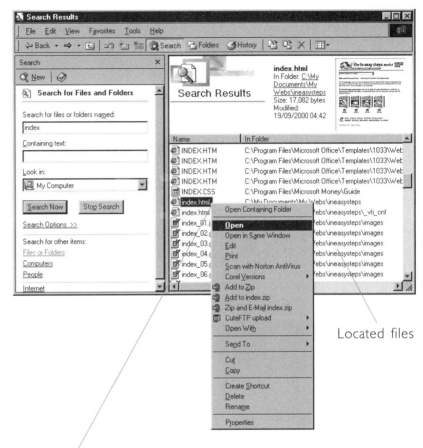

Located files

Right-click on a file. Then click on Open to edit the file in the program associated with it; Delete to erase it; Rename to amend the file's title; Copy to copy the file; Cut to copy and delete it; or Properties to view/alter its attributes.

Compressed Folders

This feature allows you to save disk space by compressing files/folders whilst still allowing them to be treated as normal folders by Windows. Compressed folders are distinguished from other folders by a zipper on the standard folder icon.

 You may not have the Compressed Folders feature installed. Run Windows Setup (see page 51) and select it as part of the System Tools component to use it.

Creating a compressed folder

 To create a compressed folder on the desktop, right-click on the desktop and then from the shortcut menu select New, Compressed Folder.

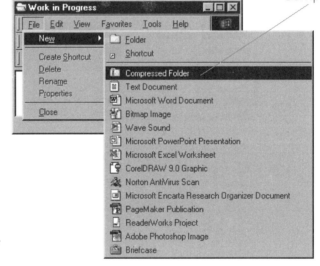

From any folder window click on File, New, Compressed Folder.

 To create a compressed folder and copy a file into it at the same time: right-click a file, select Send To, Compressed Folder. The newly created compressed folder takes the same file name as the file copied (and therefore compressed) into it, but with a file extension of .zip.

2 New Compressed Folder is created. Rename, Move, or Delete it in the same way as any other folder – as described earlier in this chapter.

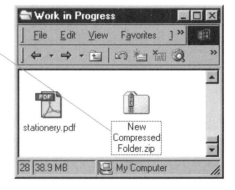

You can open a compressed folder in the same way as any other (by double-clicking on it).
   Note however, that a compressed folder window doesn't have the Up or Back Standard Buttons on the toolbar.

Adding files/folders to a compressed folder

Simply drag any files or folders into a compressed folder and they will automatically be compressed there. The original files/folders will remain – they cannot be moved to a compressed folder, but rather they are copied. If you don't need the original files you can delete them.

Extracting files/folders from a compressed folder

Again, drag the files/folders selected out of the compressed folder and they'll be decompressed. A compressed version will still remain in the compressed folder. To extract all files/folders from a compressed folder right-click on it and then click on Extract All.

You can share Compressed Folders with other users. They are compatible with other zip compression programs, like Winzip.

Encrypting a compressed folder

Right-click on a compressed folder and then click on Encrypt (or if the compressed folder is open click on File, Encrypt). In the Password box type a password and then confirm it.

Then, the password is required to open or extract any files/folders from the compressed folder. Any extracted files are automatically decrypted at the destination. However, the version remaining in the compressed folder remains encrypted unless you specifically decrypt them by choosing Decrypt either via the File menu or right-clicking the compressed folder.

Encryption will make it safer if you're sharing your files with other users on a network or emailing them. Only the people you give the password to will be able to open them.

Compressed Item Properties

Right-click on any file/folder in the compressed folder and choose Properties to see the compressed (or packed) size. Alternatively, you can compare the file sizes in the Details View (see page 61).

Creating Scraps

A 'scrap' is a piece of text copied/moved into a folder or onto the desktop, so that it can be used somewhere else by a simple drag operation. This technique serves the same purpose as the Cut, Copy and Paste operations described in Chapter 3, but it is more intuitive.

Keep the Shift key pressed when dragging the text block out to Move it instead of Copying.

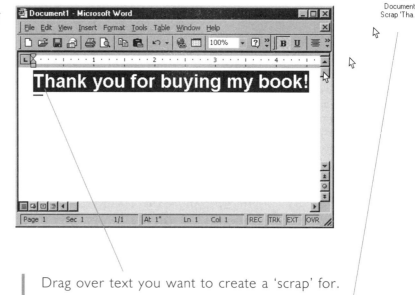

Document Scrap 'Tha...

| Drag over text you want to create a 'scrap' for.

2 Drag the block of text onto the desktop or into a folder. A Document Scrap icon is created there automatically.

Drag the Document Scrap icon onto the Recycle Bin icon to delete it, when no longer required.

3 Drag the newly created Document Scrap into another document as required and its contents will be copied there.

The Internet and the Web

In this chapter you'll set up your Internet connection using Windows ME. You'll also discover different ways to browse the web and use the latest version of Internet Explorer (V5.5) bundled with Windows ME.

Covers

Chapter Six

Internet Connection Setup

As an alternative you can run the connection software supplied by your Internet Service Provider (ISP).

Click on the Start button, Settings, Dial-Up Networking.

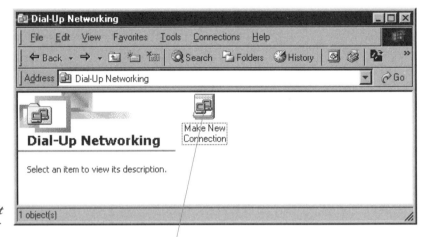

To set up your Internet connection for the first time and if you don't have your ISP's software for some reason, run the Internet Connection Wizard from the Start menu, Programs, Accessories, Communications.

2 Double-click on the Make New Connection icon.

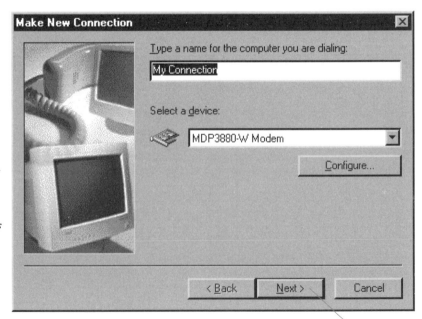

Try out MSN and other online services (includes America Online, AT&T WorldNet Service, EarthLink Internet Services, Prodigy Internet) by double-clicking on the relevant icons from the Windows ME desktop.

3 Type in any name for your connection icon and click Next.

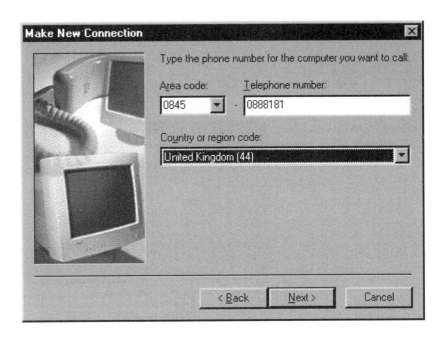

After step 4 your new Internet connection icon is set up in Dial-Up Networking. Double-click on it to connect to the Internet – see page 98.

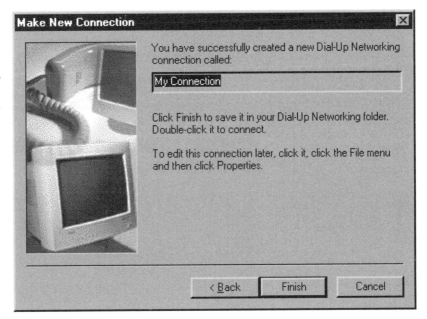

4 Type the Internet access telephone number as provided by your ISP and click Next. Finally click on Finish.

Starting your Internet Connection

Create a shortcut of your Internet connection icon from Dial-Up Networking to the Desktop for quick easy access (see page 41).

Double-click on your Internet connection icon from Dial-Up Networking as set up on pages 96-97.

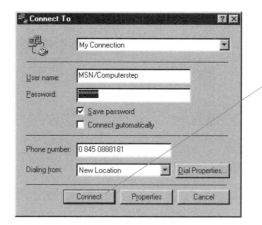

2 Type in your User name and Password (should only need to do it first time if saved). Then click on Connect.

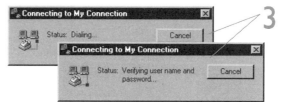

3 Monitor the progress of your connection.

To disconnect, double-click on this icon created in the taskbar:

Then click on the Disconnect button.

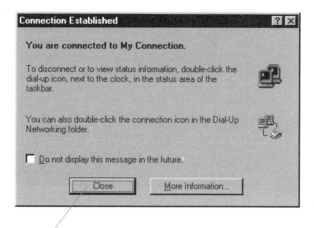

4 When connected click on the Close button.

Starting Internet Explorer

Internet Explorer

1 Double-click on the Internet Explorer icon from the desktop, choose it from Start, Programs, or from the Quick Launch toolbar.

2 Click on the Connect button from the Connect To dialog box as on previous page. This box will only appear if you're NOT connected to the Internet already.

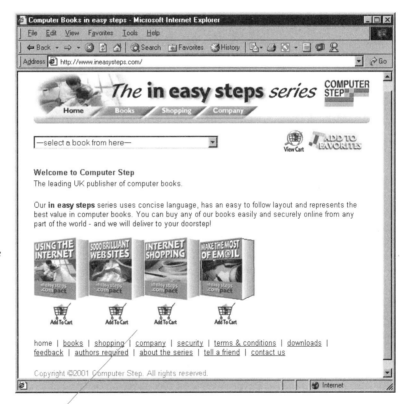

Right-click on the Internet Explorer icon from the desktop and choose Properties from the shortcut menu to customise your Internet settings (or double-click on Internet Options icon from the Control Panel).

3 The default Home page will be displayed in the browser window (Choose Tools, Internet Options to change it).

A link can be a graphic or text. Text links are usually underlined and in a different colour.

4 Browse other web pages by clicking on (hyper)links – your mouse pointer changes to a hand when rested over a link.

Browsing via the Address bar

Every page on the web has a unique address, called a URL (Uniform Resource Locator) or simply a web address. You see them advertised everywhere – newspapers, magazines and on television. To display a web page:

If you just type 'ineasysteps' and press Ctrl+Enter, the rest of the address is added for you.

| Click in the Address bar and type the url of the website you want to visit. Then press the Enter key or click on Go.

Read Internet Explorer 5.5 in easy steps book to help you use all the Internet features available to you in Windows ME.

Internet Explorer assumes that your web page starts with http:// at the beginning so you don't have to type this part in. So, for example, to visit Microsoft's home page, just enter: www.microsoft.com.

AutoComplete

When you type in an address, Windows tries to finish it based on sites you've visited before. In this way, typing:

www.i

Page 65 provides basic information on how to use the Address bar.

(for example) as above is likely to suggest addresses you may want to visit in a drop-down list – click on one that may apply. If the drop-down list is quite big you can ignore it and continue typing a bit more of the address to automatically shrink the drop-down list. This may make the selection a little easier.

You can click on the down-arrow next to the address box at any time for a list of addresses you've entered recently.

To turn off Autocomplete click on the Tools menu, select Internet Options, Content tab, AutoComplete button.

Browsing via the Links bar

The Links bar (also see page 66) provides buttons for popular websites.

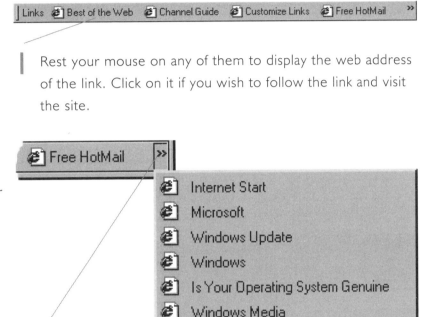

If you don't find the links buttons useful right-click on them and select Delete from the shortcut menu.

Then, to add your own links, the easiest way is to drag the page icon from the current web page address displayed in the Address bar to the Links bar.

1 Rest your mouse on any of them to display the web address of the link. Click on it if you wish to follow the link and visit the site.

2 To reveal all the links set up, click on the double arrows and select from the menu.

Browsing via the Radio bar

The new Radio bar allows you to access and listen to any radio station from your computer. This has already been covered on page 67.

Link to Radio Station Guide

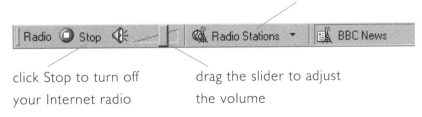

click Stop to turn off your Internet radio

drag the slider to adjust the volume

Using the Standard Browser buttons

Some of the buttons on the Standard toolbar change when you access the internet as mentioned ealier on page 64. There we covered the buttons displayed when you are just browsing local files and folders on your computer.

The most useful Internet standard buttons are:

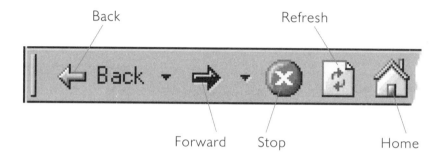

Back   Refresh

Forward   Stop   Home

Use the History bar to revisit pages – see page 106.

Back	–	Return to the page you just left. Click on the little down-arrow to the right to display a list from which you can select to go back several pages
Forward	–	Once you've gone back a few pages you may want to go forward again. To go forward several pages click on the arrow to the right.
Stop	–	Click this button to abort downloading of a slow page so you can look at something else.
Refresh	–	Click this button to reload the page to ensure that you're seeing the very latest version.
Home	–	If you really get lost click this button and it will return you to the default Home page set up when you start Internet Explorer.

Bookmark Websites using Favorites

Favorites are sites you've previously visited and deemed worthy of revisiting. Note that it's spelled in American rather than as 'Favourites' in English.

1 Click on the Favorites button from the standard toolbar or select it from View, Explorer bar.

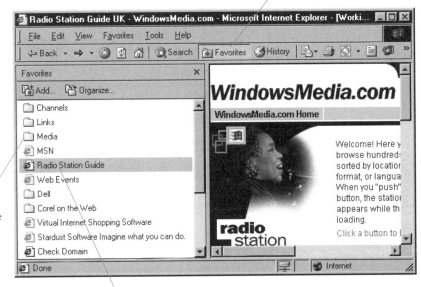

Click on a folder to access more entries.

2 Click on a Favorite.

Creating Your Own Favorites

To add the current page to your list of favorites, click on Add... at the top of the Favorites bar. In the dialog box click on OK.

Some websites will invite you to click on a link to add their page to your favorites listing. For example, go to www.ineasysteps.com and click on:

Searching the Internet

Search can also be started by clicking on the Start button, Search, On the Internet.

1 Click on the Search button from the standard toolbar or select it from View, Explorer bar.

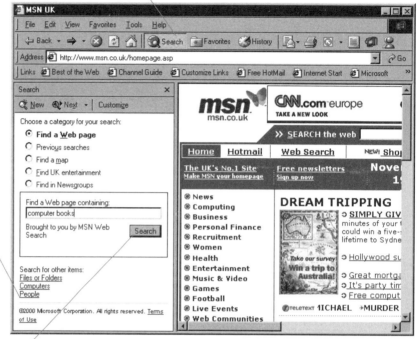

To locate people on the Web, click here (or Start button, Search, People. In the Find People dialog, type in details of the person you want to find (e.g. name). In the Look in: field, select a directory service (e.g. Yahoo! People Search). Click on Find Now.

2 Click on an option to select what you want to find and then type the word or a phrase you want to find. Click on the Search button.

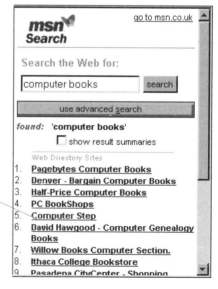

Select Tools, Show Related Links to list sites that have something in common with the current one.

3 Scroll through the results displayed. Click on any link to load its page in the right pane.

Using a different Search Engine

If you don't find what you're looking for try another search engine. Click on the little arrow near the Next button to select another one from a menu. Your keywords will be sent there automatically.

Customising the Search

Click on the Customize button to alter the search engines that are used to carry-out your searches. You may have a preference rather than using the ones Microsoft have given.

Click here to use your own preferred search engine.

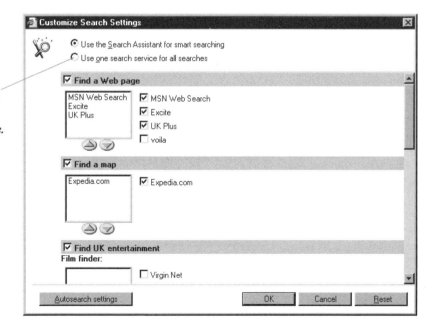

History bar

1 Click on the History button from the standard toolbar or select it from View, Explorer bar.

You can change how long the history is kept. Go to Tools, Interent Options. From the General tab alter the 'Days to keep pages in history'.

From here you can also click on the Clear History button to wipe off all the current history pages.

2 Click on a day (in history) and then on a web page to redisplay it in the right pane.

Click on Search to find a page from your history list covering a particular subject.

If you can't find the page you wanted try sorting the history list a different way by clicking on View.

Using Email

This chapter introduces Outlook Express – the email program included with Windows ME – to send and receive electronic mail.

Covers

Chapter Seven

Starting Outlook Express

Mail you receive is stored in the Inbox. Mail waiting to be sent is stored in the Outbox. Mail which has been despatched is to be found in the Sent Items folder. Messages you've deleted are kept in the Deleted Items folder.

You can use Outlook Express to:

- send e-mail

- receive e-mail

- maintain a comprehensive contact database

Customise Outlook Express via Tools, Options...

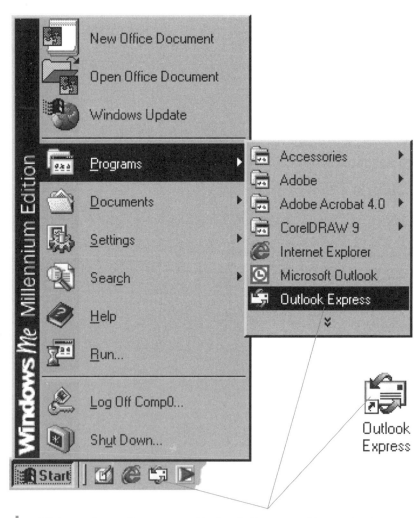

| Click on Start, Programs, Outlook Express. Alternatively, double-click on it from the desktop shortcut icon or click on it from the Quick Launch icon on the taskbar.

Setting up Accounts

Before you can use Outlook Express to send and receive email, you must:

A. set up a mail account

B. run the Internet Connection wizard

Outlook Express is a cut-down version of the main Microsoft Outlook product. Detailed coverage of both is in the book, Outlook 2000 in easy steps.

C. connect to your service provider (if you didn't do this when you started Outlook Express)

Step A leads automatically to step B and only needs to be done once initially. Step C has to be carried out every time before you can send/receive email.

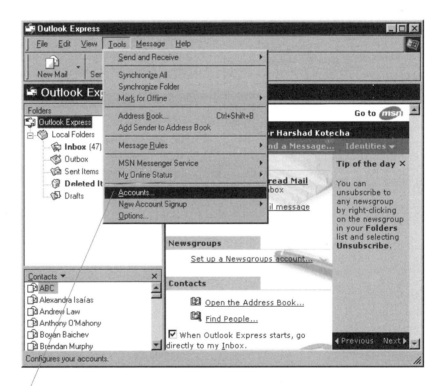

Click on Tools, then Accounts.

...cont'd

Read "Make the Most of Em@il in easy steps .compact" to learn all that you'll need to.

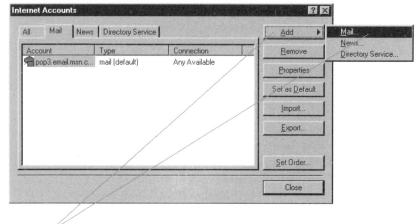

2 Click on Add, Mail...

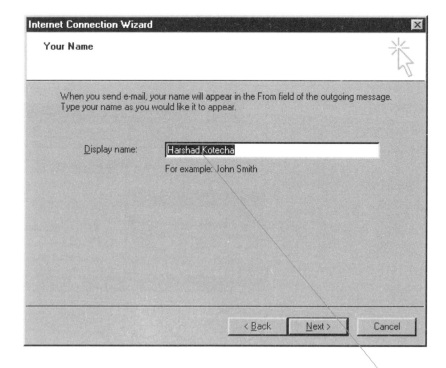

3 The Internet Connection wizard launches. Type in the name you want to appear in your email. Then click on Next.

...cont'd

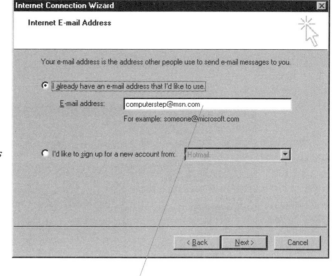

*Step 5 –
Outlook Express
currently
supports these
mail servers:*

- *POP3*
- *IMAP*
- *HTTP*

4 Type in your email address. Then click on Next.

*Step 6 –your
service provider
will supply this
information.*

5 Click on the arrow, then select a mail server.

*You may well
find that you'll
also have to
change TCP/IP
file protocols*
(activate the Network icon
in Control Panel, then select
TCP/IP) – your service
provider will advise.

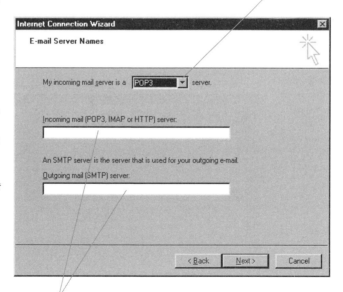

6 Complete these fields. Then click on Next. Complete the remaining dialogs and finally click on Finish.

Checking your Mail

Mail which is sent to you is stored by your service provider, and downloaded to you when you log on.

| Start Outlook Express and then click on Send/Recv.

 Click on the arrow next to the Send/Recv button and select Receive All if you don't have anything to send.

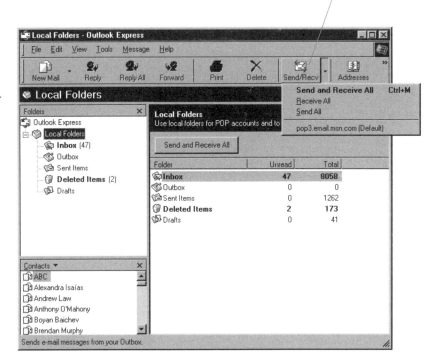

 Outgoing mail is stored in the Outbox, and sent in the same log on session as incoming mail is delivered. It's then kept in Sent Items.

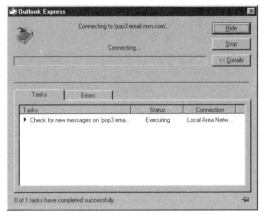

2 A connection box and a sign-in box appear. Confirm connection to your service provider, after checking your User Name and Password.

Reading Messages

Downloaded messages are stored in your Inbox.

Note the following icons to the left of messages:

The message is unread (note that the message entry is in bold).

The message has been read (the entry is in light type).

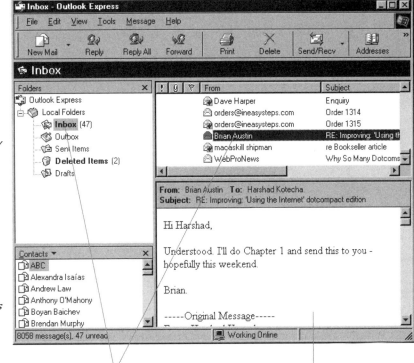

By default, Outlook Express marks a message as 'read' when it has been previewed for 5 seconds.

1   Click on Inbox. Then click on the message you want to read.

The Preview window

To delete a message, follow step 1. Then drag the message to the Deleted Items folder in the left pane.

2   Scroll through your message in the Preview window.

Reading mail with the special editor

This is an alternative way to read your mail.

1 Click on Inbox. Then double-click on the message you want to read.

Displays previous message   Displays next message

To print your message on the default printer, click on the Print button.
Choose Print... from the File menu for the Print dialog box.

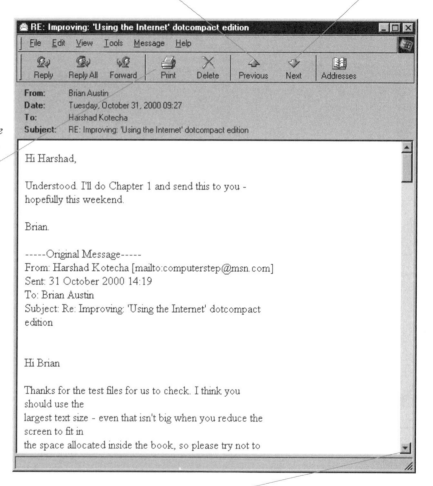

2 Scroll through your message.

3 Click on the Close window button when you've finished.

Replying to a Message

Step 2 – to send the reply to all the recipients of the message you were reading, click on the Reply All button instead:

To attach a file to a message, click on this button:

Then select a file from the Insert Attachment dialog. Finally, click on Attach.

To forward a message, follow step 1. Click on the Forward button:

Carry out steps 3-4.

I Open a message in the Preview window or the special editor (see pages 113–114).

2 Click on the Reply button in the toolbar.

4 Click on Send button (or select Send Message from the File menu).

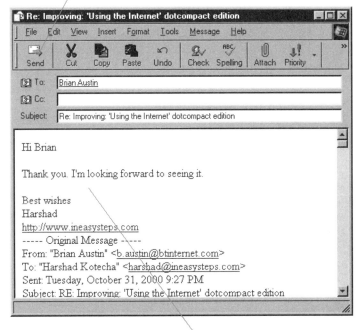

3 Type your reply here.

Batching Messages

If you have several messages to send, it's economical to batch them all together and send them with only one connection to your service provider. To batch messages in Outbox, select the Send Later option from the File menu. Then, when you're ready, send them all – see page 112.

Composing a New Message

Click on the arrow to the right of the button for a list of 'stationery' (message style) options. Click on a stationery. Then follow steps 2-4, as appropriate.

| Click on the New Mail button (available in any Outlook Express folder except the editor).

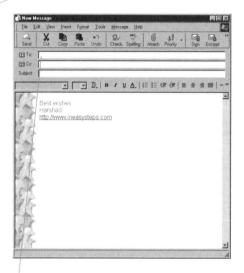

This message uses the 'Ivy' stationery

2 Type the name of the recipient and click the Check Names button or click on the To: button to launch the Address book (and follow steps 3-4).

To launch Address Book click on this button:

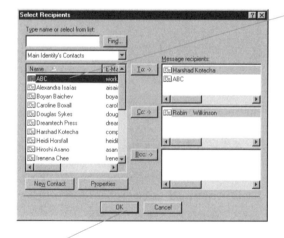

3 Select name and click on the To & Cc (courtesy copy) buttons to add as many names as you want.

4 Click on OK and follow steps 3–4 on page 115.

Printing with Windows

Whether you want a hard copy of documents you've created using an application (Word, Excel, etc.), or you want to print information from the web or your email messages, you'll need a printing capability.

This chapter shows you everything you need to know about printing under Windows ME.

Covers

Chapter Eight

Printer Setup

Before you set up your printer to work with Windows, ensure that it is connected to your computer and make a note of the printer manufacturer and model number.

 A Network printer can be set up instead of a local one through the Add Printer wizard.

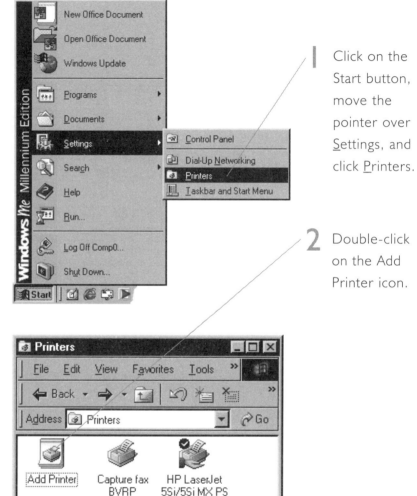

| Click on the Start button, move the pointer over Settings, and click Printers.

2 Double-click on the Add Printer icon.

 If you have more than one printer installed, choose which one should be the default – right-click on its icon and select Set as Default. This then becomes the printer your applications use automatically.

3 The Add Printer Wizard starts (see Chapter 1, Page 22). Follow the instructions to add an icon for your new printer.

Fonts

All the fonts installed on your computer are usually stored in one place: C:\WINDOWS\FONTS. To access the Fonts folder, click on Start, <u>S</u>ettings, <u>C</u>ontrol Panel. Then double-click on this icon.

You can also add new fonts by selecting <u>F</u>ile, Install New Font.

You can manage these fonts easily by treating them as files. For example, you can add new fonts by dragging them to the Fonts folder, delete old ones by deleting them from here, etc... (see Chapter 5 for full details on all File operations).

Another useful feature is that you can preview any font before you decide to use it:

Change the display for further information about fonts.
For instance, if you click on the List Fonts By <u>S</u>imilarity option from the <u>V</u>iew menu, and then use the <u>L</u>ist fonts by similarity to: drop-down box to select a base font – Windows tells you which fonts resemble it.

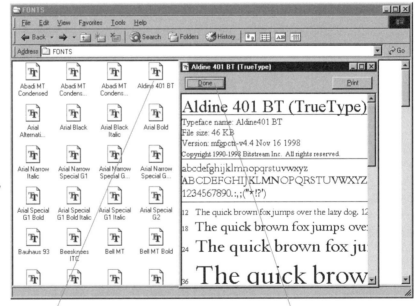

1 Right-click on the font you want to preview, then click on <u>O</u>pen in the shortcut menu.

2 A preview of the selected font is displayed. Click on <u>P</u>rint or <u>D</u>one.

Printing Documents

Once your printer is set up in Windows, printing is easy. You can print a document from the Program that created it or by dragging the file onto the Printer icon.

From the menu

Click on this icon:

in the toolbar to quickly print one copy of the whole document to the default printer set up, and thus avoid the Print dialog box altogether.

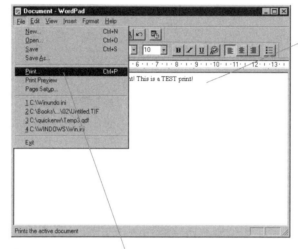

| Type in some text in your application, or open a document you want to print.

2 Click on File and then Print...

Select Print Preview from the File menu first to ensure your document will print as expected.

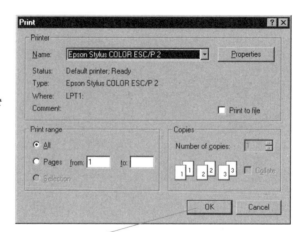

3 Click on OK after amending the options, if required (e.g. pages to print, no. of copies).

Using drag-and-drop

Avoid having too many printers. When you buy a new printer delete the setup for the old one – right-click on its icon and select Delete.

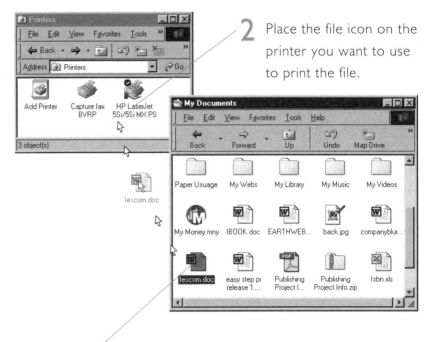

2 Place the file icon on the printer you want to use to print the file.

Drag out a file you want to print.

You can have a shortcut icon for a specific printer rather than the actual printer icon – if you are going to use the drag-and-drop technique often, create a shortcut icon for your main printer on the desktop (See page 41).

Once you've dragged-and-dropped a file onto the printer icon, the program associated with the file is started and so is the printing – automatically!

Print Management

It is easy to find out which documents are currently printing and which are still waiting in the queue. Also shown is the document name, owner, size and when the print job was submitted.

You can pause, resume or cancel your print jobs submitted on a network printer attached to another PC. It isn't necessary to walk to the PC the printer is attached to.

You can also double-click the small printer icon displayed on the taskbar after a print job is submitted to display the print queue and status of your print jobs.

Double-click on the printer icon your jobs are submitted to.

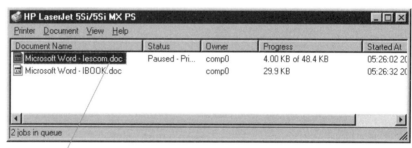

Document Name	Status	Owner	Progress	Started At
Microsoft Word - lescom.doc	Paused - Pri...	comp0	4.00 KB of 48.4 KB	05:26:02 20
Microsoft Word - IBOOK.doc		comp0	29.9 KB	05:26:32 20

2 jobs in queue

2 Click on the job you want to change the status of. Here Pause Printing from the Document menu was selected. This allows a job further down the queue to print before. Click on Pause Printing again to resume printing.

Click on Pause Printing from the Printer menu to make the printer pause e.g. to change the paper type.

Note that whenever there is a problem (e.g. a paper jam), the small printer icon on the Taskbar displays a red warning circle with a question mark. Move your mouse over it for an

explanation, or double-click on it to display the print queue again (so that you can resume printing after correcting any problems.)

Configuration

You can configure many of your printer settings depending on the type of printer you have.

1 From the Printers folder, right-click once on the printer icon you want to configure.

2 In the shortcut menu, click on Properties.

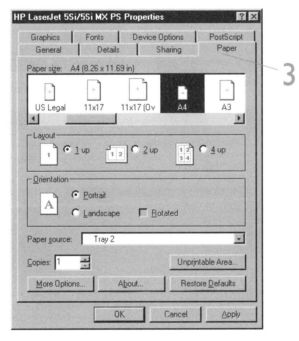

3 Click on the appropriate tab and change the settings, as required. Finally, click on OK.

Click on the Print Test Page button (from the General tab) after you have first installed your printer to ensure that it works as expected. If it doesn't, Windows will guide you through correcting the problem.

The Restore Defaults button is available from most tab settings so if you really make a mess of things, just click on this button.

Troubleshooting

Printing problems are common. If you experience difficulties, use the Windows Help system to resolve them.

1 Click on the Start button and then on <u>H</u>elp.

2 Click on the Index tab.

See pages 18-19 for an example of a slightly different way of starting the Printing Troubleshooter.

3 Type "printing tr" in the box. Ensure "Printing troubleshooter" is selected.

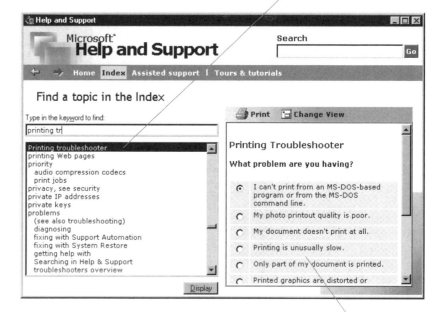

4 Click on the Display button. Then follow the instructions in the right pane of the window.

Home Networking

A *network* is a group of computers linked together. There is a built-in basic networking capability within Windows ME allowing you to share files, printers and an Internet connection between two or more computers in your home.

Before you can set networking up, ensure that your computers have *network adapters* (also known as Network Interface Cards – NIC) installed. These control the communication of one computer with another in the network. The computers also need to be physically connected, via the network adpters, using special cables and connectors.

Covers

Chapter Nine

Home Networking Wizard

Click on the Start button, Programs, Accessories, Communications, Home Networking Wizard.

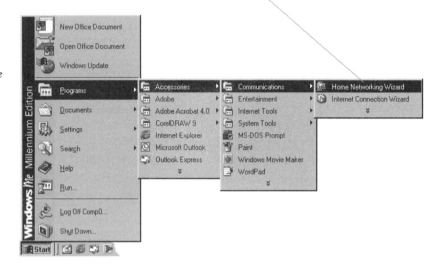

Run the Home Networking Wizard from each of the computers in your Network.

Click Next on all the Wizard dialogs that follow after making your choices. Finally click on Finish.

2 Click Next to begin setting up your network.

The Home Networking Wizard also sets up Internet Connection Sharing (ICS). If you have not yet signed up with an ISP (Internet Service Provider), you might want to do that first.

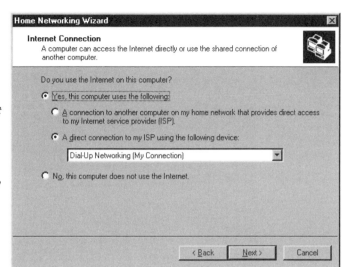

3   If your computer connects to the Internet, choose how?

If your Network Interface Card doesn't appear in the drop-down list, then the chances are it hasn't been installed properly. Click on Cancel and sort out the hardware before returning to the Home Networking Wizard.

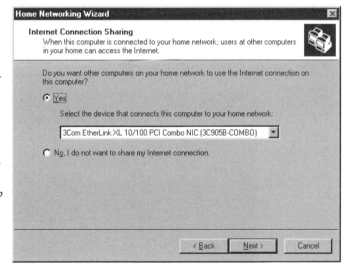

4   If asked, choose whether you want to allow others on the network to share your Internet connection. If you do, select the NIC in your computer if it doesn't appear already.

ICS allows all PCs in a network to browse the web and use email simultaneously, with just one PC having an Internet connection (provided it's turned on).

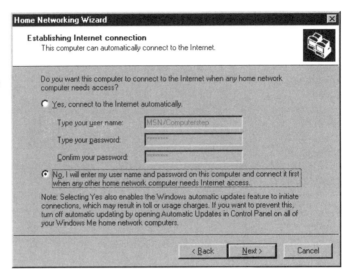

5 If asked, decide if you want others on the network to force an Internet connection from this computer, or do you want to establish it first specifically before allowing others access.

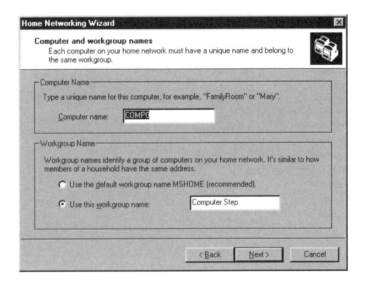

6 Specify a name to identify this PC in the network. The workgroup name should be the same for all the computers.

...cont'd

If you don't want to give access to your files to all the users in the network, specify a password and then give that to just the people you trust. e.g your partner but not your kids.

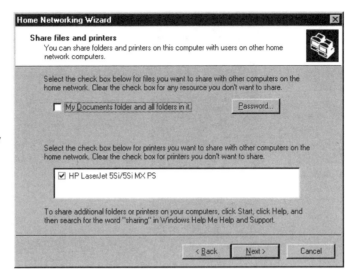

7 Click on the check box to share the files in My Documents main folder (and in all the other folders that may contain) with other networked computers. Also select the printer(s) to share.

A program file called setup.exe will be created on a floppy disk if you create a setup disk. Run this program from the other w95/w98 computers to complete your home networking setup.

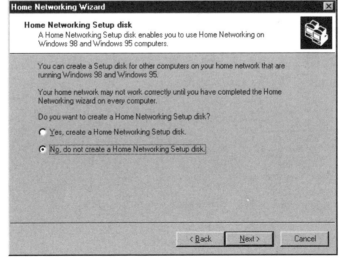

8 Create a setup disk if other computers use Windows 95/98.

...cont'd

The Home Networking Wizard modifies some important system files. If you don't restart your computer when prompted and continue using Windows, you could experience problems.

Home Networking Wizard

Completing the Home Networking wizard

The Home Networking wizard is ready to make any changes you specified.

If you created or used a Home Networking wizard Setup disk, remove the disk from the floppy drive.

If you need help using your home network, see Windows Me Help and Support. Click Start, click Help, click Home Networking, and then click Using Home Networking.

To close this wizard, click Finish. If you are prompted to restart your computer, click Yes.

< Back   Finish   Cancel

You can always run the Home Networking Wizard again to change any of the settings.

9 Click on the Finish button. Windows should then prompt you to restart your computer. Click Yes to restart. When Windows comes back on, it should confirm that Home Networking has been set up successfully on this computer.

My Network Places

Once your network is set up, use My Network Places to easily browse at any shared information on other computers. It's very similar to My Computer (page 56) which shows local files in your PC.

All the shared folders/drives in your home network appear from here (see next screenshot) for quick and direct access.
Note that the computers they belong to must be switched on.

My Network Places

Double-click on the My Network Places icon from the desktop.

...cont'd

Double-click here to create additional paths to shared folders, a web folder on the Internet, or an FTP site, so they also appear in My Network Places.

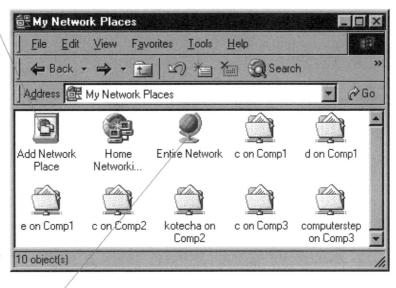

In Folders View (any window) there is an entry in the left pane for My Network Places too – you can also access the whole network from here.

2 Double-click on the Entire Network icon.

3 Double-click on the workgroup name used for your network.

Your own computer appears here too. Double-clicking on a computer icon not only shows each shared drive and any individually shared folders, but also any network printers that may be attached – double-click on the printer icon to manage your print (see page 122).

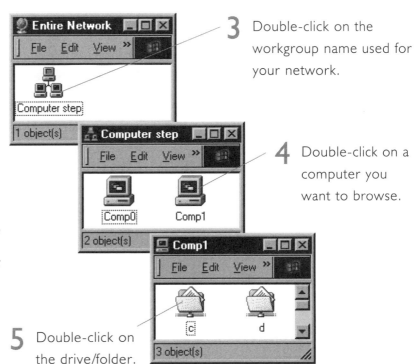

4 Double-click on a computer you want to browse.

5 Double-click on the drive/folder.

Sharing your Folders and Printers

Check that there is an entry for 'File and printer sharing for Microsoft Networks' in the Network components installed listing (via Control Panel, Network). If not, click on the 'File and Print Sharing...' button.

To be able to share your files you need to share the folder they are in. You can also share the printer(s) attached to your computer with other users networked to your computer. If you didn't share everything you wanted to in the Home Network Networking Wizard, or if you want to share additional folders/printers follow the steps below:

To share a folder

To share all the files and folders in your entire local disk drive C, right-click on its icon instead of a folder.

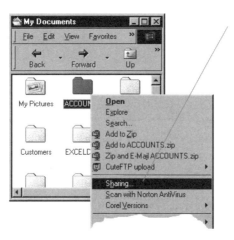

Right-click on the folder you want to share. Then click on the Sharing...

A little hand appears below the folder icon to indicate that it is shared:

2 From the Sharing tab, click on the Shared As option.

3 Select Full if you want to allow others to update your files and type password(s), if appropriate.

...cont'd

To share your printer

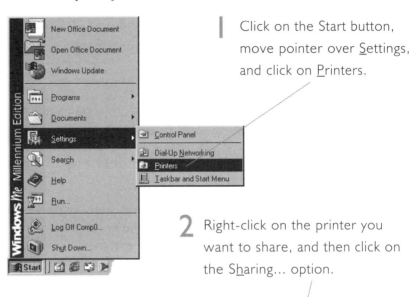

1 Click on the Start button, move pointer over Settings, and click on Printers.

2 Right-click on the printer you want to share, and then click on the Sharing... option.

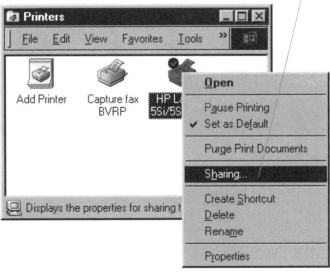

Before you can use a shared printer set up on another computer on the network, you will need to set it up again on your computer as a Network printer (See page 118 Printer Setup). Then print your documents as normal using the new network printer.

3 In the Printer Properties box click on the Shared As option, specify a password if necessary and then click OK. A little hand appears below the printer icon.

HP LaserJet
5Si/5Si MX PS

Using Shared Resources from other Computers

Create a shortcut on your desktop to a network resource, like a drive or printer, you use frequently from My Network Places. See Creating a Shortcut, Page 41.

Once a folder or a disk from another networked computer is shared (see previous topic), you can access it from My Network Places icon (see earlier topic). Simply open the folder from the other computer to use the files it contains.

If you are frequently going to use the same shared folder, then it is best to assign a logical drive letter to it (e.g. E, F, G, ...). Then, you can access it from My Computer or Windows Explorer in exactly the same way as any of your own physical drives.

Logical drives don't really exist – you are mapping, say, a folder on the hard disk C in another computer to a logical drive F on your computer. You cannot map it as the same letter C because you already use it for your own hard disk drive. You can use several letters to map different folders from one or more other computers you are connected to.

After you've mapped a network drive its icon appears in My Computer. Use files from here as if it's your own local drive. Note that it has a small cable at the base of the icon to distinguish it from your local drives.

C on 'Comp3'
(F:)

1 Click on the Map Drive icon in the Standard Buttons toolbar from any window. If the Map Drive (and the associated Disconnect) icons aren't there, right-click on the toolbar, select Customize, and add them. You can also map onto shared drives by right-clicking on My Computer or My Network Places.

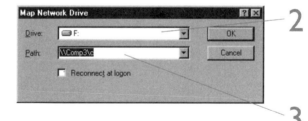

2 The next free drive letter appears here.

3 Type in the path for the folder (including the computer name).

You can also right-click on a connected drive icon and select Disconnect.

4 Click here when you've finished using the shared drive.

Customising your Windows

This chapter shows you how to change the way Windows ME looks on your computer and how to alter other settings to suit your requirements. Additionally, you'll learn to set up Windows ME for multiple users. Finally, there is also advice for users with special needs.

Covers

Chapter Ten

Colours

If you have desktop themes installed (Windows Setup, page 51) you can change the *colours, wallpaper, mouse pointer, icons, screen saver, etc. to follow one of the available themes e.g. Baseball, Space. To set up one of these themes, double-click on the Desktop Themes icon from the Control Panel.*

You can change most of the colours you see in Windows and Windows applications to suit your taste. You can't however change the colours of the icons.

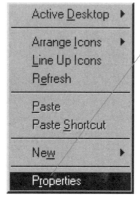

1 Right-click on any free space on the desktop. Then click on Properties from the shortcut menu displayed.

You can also change the number of colours your monitor displays and the resolution via the Settings tab.

Resolution is measured in pixels or the number of picture elements displayed. The higher this number is the sharper the picture becomes, but it also gets smaller.

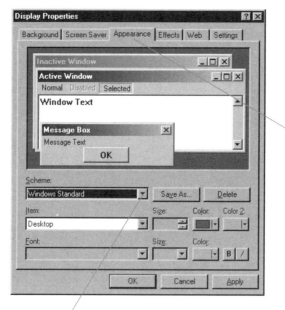

2 Click on the Appearance tab.

3 Click on this down-arrow and click on another colour Scheme from the list displayed. The preview for it appears on top. Click on OK. You can also change individual items (colour, size, font) instead of the whole scheme.

Wallpapers and Patterns

Using a Wallpaper for your desktop

You can change the desktop background with a colourful wallpaper of your choice.

| Right-click on any free space on the desktop. Then click on Properties from the shortcut menu displayed.

Picture Display options: Center displays a wallpaper once in the centre, Tile and Stretch fill the whole desktop – either by repeating the basic design or stretching it.

Click on the Browse... button to locate other images to use as wallpapers, including HTML (web) pages.

2 Click on the Background tab. Then click on a wallpaper you like. Finally, click on OK.

Using a Pattern for your desktop

A Pattern is a series of dots repeated. You cannot use both a Wallpaper and a Pattern. So to select a background pattern, first ensure None is chosen as the Wallpaper.

Wallpapers and Patterns may slow down your computer. To deselect them, just choose None.

| Click on the Pattern... button, select a pattern in the Pattern dialog, then click on OK. Click OK again from the Display Properties box.

Screen Savers

Screen savers are images displayed on the screen when there is no activity for some time. This was supposed to prevent older monitors from *burn in*. Nowadays they're used for fun.

Right-click on any free space on the desktop. Then click on Properties from the shortcut menu displayed.

Click here to vary the default variables of a screen saver (e.g. colours, speed, size) and depends on the particular screen saver chosen.

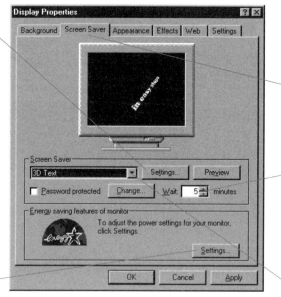

2 Click on the Screen Saver tab.

3 Change the period of inactivity before the screen saver starts.

Click here to set Power Options properties – ensure Turn off monitor is set to: Never. Otherwise the Screen saver may never start but instead your monitor switches off temporarily (also see page 180).

4 Click on the pull-down arrow and select a Screen Saver. Click on the Preview button to see the screen saver in action. To continue working after a screen saver display, press any key or move your mouse a little.

Multiple Users

See page 24 for how to log off so another user can use your PC.

Rerun the wizard as many times as there are users.

At the end of the process, Windows restarts. When prompted, log on by typing in the user name and password you set up in the wizard. Then customise your profile – changes you make are automatically saved in your name.

Windows ME has a special wizard you can run – the Enable Multi-user Settings wizard – which sets up your computer for use by more than one user. This involves:

A. setting up unique user names and passwords for each user

B. creating multiple desktop profiles (customised desktops, including Programs, Start menu, Favorites, and My Documents). Each user has his/her own profile.

1 Double-click on the Users icon from the Control Panel window (Start menu, Settings).

2 Follow the instructions given in a series of dialog boxes.

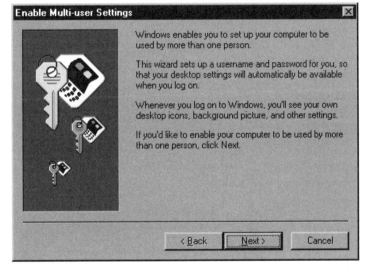

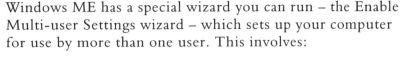

In order to create separate user profiles, you must grant permission from Control panel, Passwords, User Profiles tab.

3 Click on the Back button to change options from the previous box, or Cancel to abandon the procedure altogether. Otherwise, continue to select Next until the last box which replaces this button with Finish.

Date and Time

Your computer has an internal clock which can be reset at any time. It's usually displayed on the taskbar (bottom right corner) so you can keep track of time whilst working.

Windows date-and-time stamps every file you save so ensure they are correct.

To display the clock

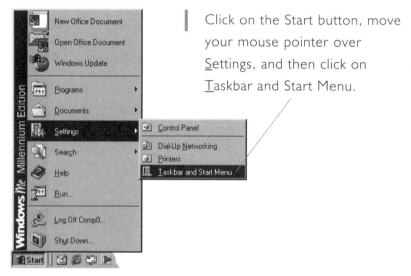

Click on the Start button, move your mouse pointer over Settings, and then click on Taskbar and Start Menu.

You can also right-click on any blank section of the Taskbar and click on Properties from the shortcut menu to produce this same window.

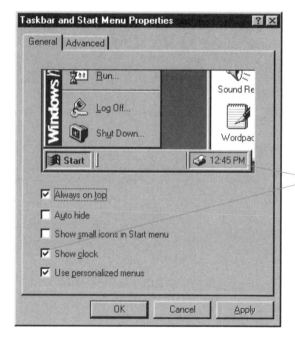

2 Click on the Show clock box so that it's ticked and displayed on the Taskbar preview. Then click on OK.

To display the date

Move your mouse pointer over the time displayed on the Taskbar and leave it there for a couple of seconds. The current date then pops up.

To reset date/time

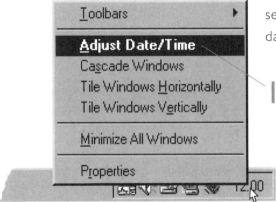

1 Right-click on the time and then click here.

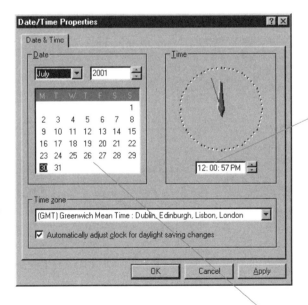

2 Click inside the HH, MM, SS or AM/PM part of the time box and either type a new value or use the arrows.

Click on the Time zone down-arrow to change the Greenwich Mean Time for another country.

3 Click on another day from the calendar and use the arrows to change the month/year above it. Finally, click on OK.

Mouse

The make of mouse attached to your computer may be different from the Microsoft IntelliPoint shown here. However, similar customising options will still be offered.

 Like your mouse, your keyboard settings can be changed to suit your personal preference. Double-click on the Keyboard icon, also in the Control Panel:

Keyboard

Mouse

| Double-click on the Mouse icon from the Control Panel window (Start menu, Settings).

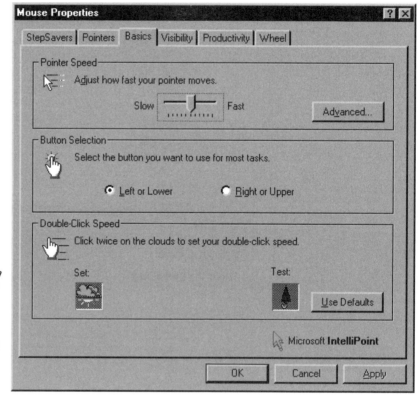

 If your PC has a USB (Universal Serial Bus) port, you can add new serial devices (e.g. mice, keyboards and modems) without having to install an adapter card, and without first switching off your machine. Windows ME automatically detects the new device and installs the necessary driver (software which runs it).

2 Change the way your mouse works and also the way the pointers look. Use other tabs to change other settings if required. Finally, click on OK.

Sounds and Multimedia

You can assign different sounds to events that occur when using Windows, like when starting Windows, when you exit Windows, and so on. These will only work, of course, if you have multimedia computer with a sound card and speakers.

Sounds and Multimedia

I Double-click on the Sounds and Multimedia icon from the Control Panel window (Start menu, Settings).

If you don't want any sound for an event, select it and then choose None in step 3.

If you have Multimedia Sound Schemes installed you'll be able to select a Scheme from the drop-down list consisting of a set of sounds e.g. Jungle Sound Scheme, Utopia Sound Scheme.

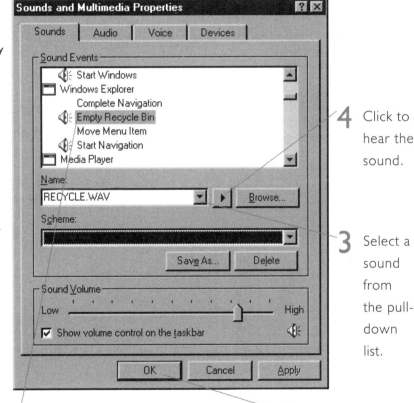

4 Click to hear the sound.

3 Select a sound from the pull-down list.

2 Click on the event you want to add/change the sound for.

5 Click here to accept the changes and close this dialog box.

Taskbar

These are the default settings. To view more toolbars, right-click on any blank section of the Taskbar. In the shortcut menu, click on Toolbars. In the sub-menu, click on a toolbar – see page 68.

The principal components of the Taskbar, usually at the bottom of the screen, are:

- the Start button

- the clock and printer status icons

- task buttons for each open application

- the Quick Launch toolbar

To move/resize the Taskbar

1 Drag the Taskbar (from a clear area) to the top, bottom, left or right screen edges.

Try not to have a large Taskbar as it will reduce your desktop space.

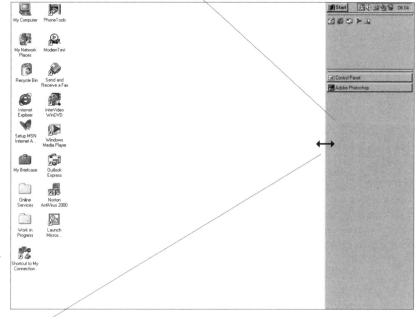

To return the Taskbar to its original location, simply drag it back.

2 Move your mouse pointer over the inside edge of the Taskbar so that it changes to a double-headed arrow. Then drag it in either direction to change the width of the Taskbar.

To change Taskbar properties

1 Right-click on any free space on the Taskbar and then click on Properties from the shortcut menu displayed. (Or click on the Start menu, move the mouse over Settings and click on Taskbar and Start Menu).

Select this to make the Taskbar disappear, giving you more desktop space.
You can still make it temporarily visible at any time by moving the mouse pointer over the relevant screen edge (depending on where the Taskbar has been located).

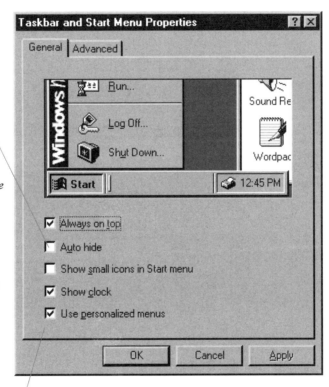

2 Click on the appropriate boxes (so that they are ticked) to turn on features, or click on ticked boxes to turn off features. Then click on OK.

Windows for the Impaired

Microsoft recognises that some users are likely to have difficulty with certain operating tasks. As a result, you can opt to make use of specific workarounds. For example, if you have trouble using a mouse (perhaps because of RSI – Repetitive Strain Injury), you can opt to use the Numeric Keypad on the right of your keyboard to mimic mouse operation. Or, if you're visually impaired, you can use the Magnifier to provide an enlargement of the screen area currently under the mouse pointer. The easiest way to set these and other options is via the Accessibility Wizard:

| Click on Start, Programs, Accessories, Accessibility, Accessibility Wizard.

As an alternative double-click on Accessibility Options in the Control Panel to change settings.

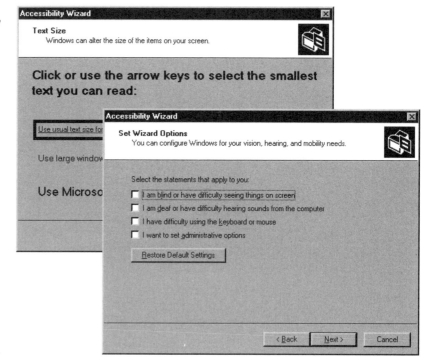

For further information and other programs visit http://www.microsoft.com/enable/

2 Complete the dialogs which launch, clicking on Next to move on to successive screens. Finally, click on Finish to complete the wizard.

Home Entertainment

Computers are not just for serious work – they're for playing too! Since this book covers the consumer version of Windows, it wouldn't be complete without covering the entertainment features of ME. These include playing games, playing and recording sounds, playing CDs and video clips using the new Media Player 7, creating home movies with Microsoft's new Movie Maker and creating your own private photo collection.

Covers

Chapter Eleven

Playing Games

Windows ME provides several games for young adults. Some of them require you to connect to the Internet.

1 Click on Start and move the mouse over Programs, then Games, and then select a game you want to play.

 If you don't see any games on your computer, they may not have been installed. Run Windows Setup (page 51) to add them.

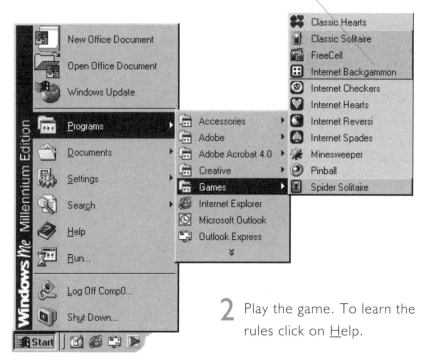

2 Play the game. To learn the rules click on Help.

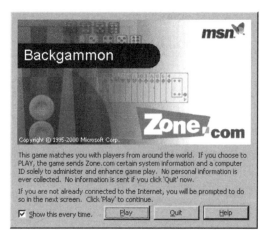

Backgammon

msn

Zone.com

Copyright © 1995-2000 Microsoft Corp.

This game matches you with players from around the world. If you choose to PLAY, the game sends Zone.com certain system information and a computer ID solely to administer and enhance game play. No personal information is ever collected. No information is sent if you click 'Quit' now.

If you are not already connected to the Internet, you will be prompted to do so in the next screen. Click 'Play' to continue.

☑ Show this every time.   Play   Quit   Help

Setting Gaming Options

You can add or modify any special game controllers you've
bought to use with your computer. e.g. a flightstick or a
gamepad.

**Gaming
Options**

| Click on Start, Settings, Control Panel and then double-click on the Gaming Options icon.

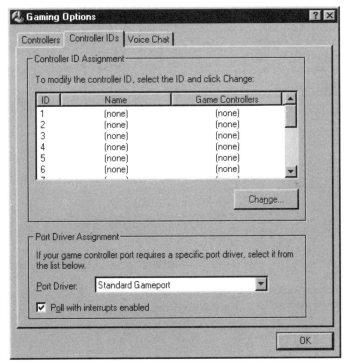

*If you're playing
a game from
an Internet web
site the host
must allow
Voice Chat to be used, and
your game opponent(s)
must also enable Voice Chat
for you to be able to talk to
them.*

*Using Voice
Chat may slow
your game
down,
depending on
the speed of your computer
and Internet connection.*

2 Use the Controllers tab to add a new game controller or to
modify the Properties of an existing one. Use the Controller
IDs tab to change the port to which you've connected your
game controller. Use the Voice chat tab to turn on the in-
game chat for games that use DirectPlay.

Volume Control

Instead of turning the knob on your speakers you can adjust the volume and balance through Windows. Apart from the speakers, you can also adjust volume for other audio devices you may have attached.

| Click on the Volume Control icon once from the taskbar

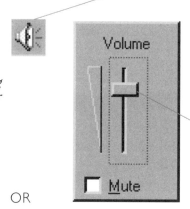

If you're playing a noisy game or listening to music and the phone rings, just click on the Mute box.

2 Drag the slider to adjust volume or click on the Mute box to kill off sound.

OR

| Double-click on the Volume Control icon from the taskbar (or click on Start, Programs, Accessories, Entertainment, Volume Control) to adjust volume settings for all your audio input and output devices.

You can choose which devices appear here for Volume Control from Options, Properties.

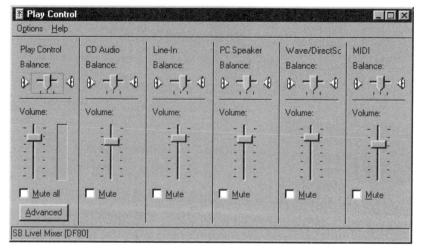

Playing and Recording Sounds

Playing different sounds and recording them can be useful and fun. For example, you can create your own sounds and link them to Windows events (see page 143).

You'll need a microphone attached to your PC if you want to record sounds.

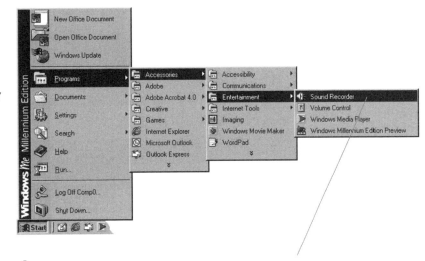

Click on Start, Programs, Accessories, Entertainment, Sound Recorder.

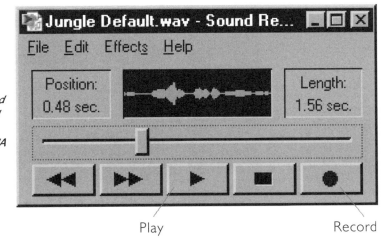

Windows sound files are stored in the folder: Windows\MEDIA if you want to try playing some of these.

Play   Record

2 Click on File, Open... to open any sound file (usually .wav file type) and then click on the Play button.

Media Player

A lot of effort has gone into the new Windows Media Player. It looks slicker and much more user-friendly. You can use it to listen to your favourite CDs in the background as you work, view video clips you created or that were sent to you by friends and family, or listen to Internet radio stations.

Media Player incorporates Digital rights – that's to say you'll be able to copy CDs and play them on your own PC and also download tracks to a portable device, but not transfer them to another PC.

Insert a music CD into your CD/DVD drive and Media Player should open and start playing the tracks automatically. If it doesn't: click Start, Programs, Accessories, Entertainment, Windows Media Player. You can also open Media Player by clicking on its icon in the Quick Launch toolbar.

Play list

Click on the CD Audio button to name the tracks in your CD. If you want help, click on the Get Names link from there and connect to the Internet to find the names.

2 Double-click on a specific track here to play it.

Media Player buttons

Media Player Visualizations are superb — they are in sync with the music playing. You can also select specific ones from the View menu, Visualizations.

Previous and Next Visualization buttons   Seek

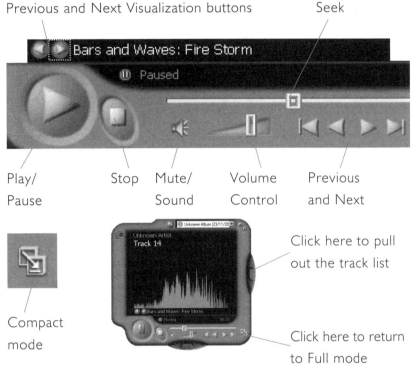

Play/
Pause   Stop   Mute/
Sound   Volume
Control   Previous
and Next

Click here to pull out the track list

Compact mode

Click here to return to Full mode

Media Player tabs

Visit http:// www.internet radiolist.com for lots of Internet radio station links.

Now Playing — To play any media from the play list

Media Guide — To access Internet media (see next page)

CD Audio — To edit and view CD track details

Media Library — To organise all your media into relevant folders

Radio Tuner — To listen to Internet radio (see also page 67)

Portable Device — To copy music to say your portable MP3 player

Skin Chooser — To select a new look for your Media Player (see next page)

Media Guide

Internet radio and other sound and video media downloaded uses 'streaming' technology – instead of downloading the whole media file (which can take a long time) before it's played, playback starts as soon as the first bit of it is downloaded. So you can start enjoying the media clip quickly whilst the rest of the file downloads in the background.

Click on the Media Guide tab and connect to the Internet. You're taken to www.windowsmedia.com as shown above. This web site is displayed in Media Player rather than your standard Internet Explorer. From here you'll be able to choose and play movie trailers, pop videos, etc. Enjoy!

Skin Chooser

Click on the Skin Chooser tab and then select and apply a skin you like. The one shown here is called Headspace. You'll also be able to download more skins from the Interent for use with Media Player.

Movie Maker

Movie Maker is very resource hungry – you'll need a fast PC and at least 2Gb of free hard disk space. You'll also need a video capture device attached.

This is a simple video editing package. It allows you to easily combine audio, video and pictures to produce your own home movies. Once you've transferred some video footage onto your PC, use Movie Maker to create your masterpiece.

Click on Start, Programs, Accessories, Windows Movie Maker.

Collections – build up and store different video clips, sound files and still images here.

Preview – play any clip in a collection here, before you decide to use it in your film.

Save your finished movie in a streaming video format compatible with Media Player. Then upload it to the Internet so your friends and family (from anywhere in the world) can view it easily.

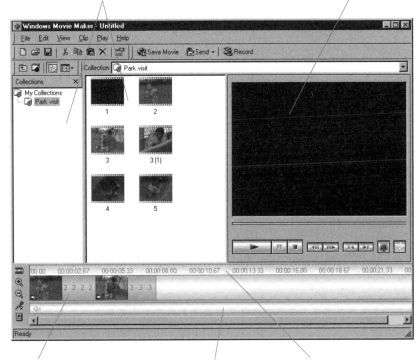

Storyboard – used to construct your film. Drag and drop video and audio clips, including pictures here.

Timeline – used to set how long individual clips should play for, and to fade in two clips together if you want to.

Soundtrack – place any audio to play over your film here.

Home Photo Album

The new My Pictures folder within My Documents is a very useful place to organise and store your holiday snaps or any other pictures.

 If you don't see the 'scanner or camera' link, Windows Plug and Play has not detected your Image input device – install it from Start, Settings, Control Panel, Scanners and Cameras, Add Device.

1 Access My Pictures folder using My Computer or Windows Explorer (see Chapter 4). Then click here to import pictures from a scanner or a digital camera.

 Once you've created your photo album or digital photo collection, send them to friends as email attachments (see page 115) or use them as your desktop wallpapers (see page 137).

 Thumbnail view here is the most useful, but you can change it to another type of view (see page 61).

2 Select a thumbnail picture and use this Image Viewer (built-in from My Pictures and all folders under it) to zoom in and out, preview at full size, print and rotate – all from its own little toolbar above.

3 Click to run a slideshow of all the pictures stored in the current folder. You can either use the toolbar there to view the slideshow, or just click to move to the next slide and the Esc key to close the slideshow.

Using Windows Accessories

Windows Accessories are basic programs and utilities provided free with Windows ME. If a program described here is not available on your computer, install the relevant Windows component (see page 51).

Covers

Chapter Twelve

WordPad

WordPad is a basic word processor used to create and edit documents.

> Click on Start and move the mouse over Programs, then Accessories, and then click on WordPad.

To edit text in WordPad, do the following, as appropriate:

- *Move the mouse pointer to the start of the text you want to edit – it will change to an I-beam. Then click on the mouse and drag it to the end of the text-string you want to edit. The selected piece of text will be highlighted.*

- *Press the Del key on your keyboard to delete the selected text, or type in some new text to replace it.*

- *Drag the selected text to another part of the text block to move it, or press the Control key when dragging to make a copy of it elsewhere.*

Open a document

Helps you find a document

Click to insert today's date (or time) in a specific format

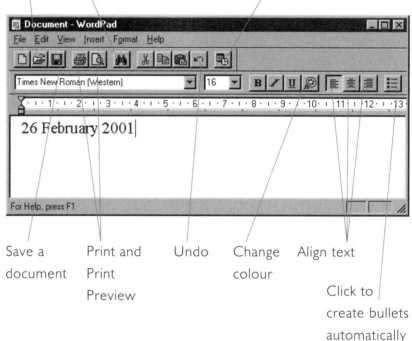

Save a document

Print and Print Preview

Undo

Change colour

Align text

Click to create bullets automatically

Creating a new document

> To create a new document, simply start typing in WordPad
>
> or
>
> Click on New... from the File menu. This will allow you to choose the type of document to create (e.g. Word) although you can specify this when you save the document. Click OK.

Paint

Paint is a basic drawing and painting program. It can also be used to enhance scanned images and digital photos.

You can use another accessory – Imaging – to edit scanned images (see page 162).

Click on Start and move the mouse over <u>P</u>rograms, then Accessories, and then click on Paint.

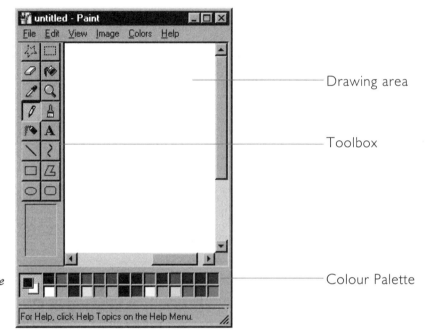

Drawing area

Toolbox

Colour Palette

To draw in Paint, select a tool (e.g. Brush). Then drag the mouse in the Drawing area. (If you make a mistake, press Ctrl+Shift+N – then start all over again.)

Toolbox

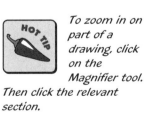
To zoom in on part of a drawing, click on the Magnifier tool. Then click the relevant section.

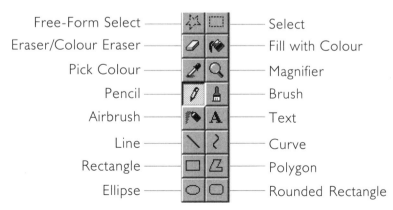

Free-Form Select — Select
Eraser/Colour Eraser — Fill with Colour
Pick Colour — Magnifier
Pencil — Brush
Airbrush — Text
Line — Curve
Rectangle — Polygon
Ellipse — Rounded Rectangle

Character Map

The Character Map enables you to use characters and special symbols from other character sets in your document.

1 Click on Start and move the mouse over Programs, Accessories, System Tools. Then click on Character Map.

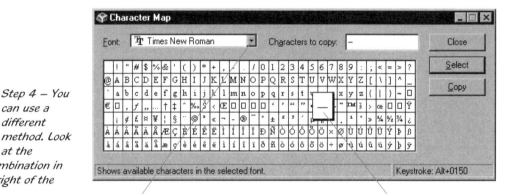

Step 4 – You can use a different method. Look at the keystroke combination in the bottom right of the dialog:

Keystroke: Alt+0150

To use this, go to the relevant document. Press the Num Lock key. Hold down Alt, and type out the numerical component (in this case, 0150) on the Numerical keypad at the right of your keyboard. Release Alt, then press Num Lock again.

2 Click and select the font from the drop-down list.

3 Click and hold down the mouse to magnify the character.

4 Double-click on a character to send it to the 'Characters to copy' box (or click on a character once and press the Select button). Repeat this for as many characters as you want to include. Then click on the Copy button to copy the character(s) in the 'Characters to copy' box to the Clipboard. From here you can paste the character(s) into your document in the normal way.

See the next topic for how to use the Clipboard.

Clipboard Viewer

The Clipboard is a temporary storage area. It is used to transfer information (text and graphics) between applications and within the same document.

Whenever you select an object/text from an application and click on Cut or Copy from the Edit menu, it goes into the Clipboard. The Print Screen button on your keyboard also copies the whole screen to the Clipboard, while Alt+Print Screen copies just the active window. To insert the contents of the Clipboard somewhere else later on, click on Paste from the Edit menu. (See Cut, Copy and Paste in Chapter 3, Working with Programs.)

It is not necessary to use Clipboard Viewer to perform the Cut, Copy and Paste functions. However, you must remember that the contents of the Clipboard are overwritten if you copy something else into it, and cleared when you quit Windows. Therefore the main benefit of using the Clipboard Viewer is to save its contents for subsequent retrieval.

1 Click on Start and move the mouse over Programs, Accessories, System Tools. Then click on Clipboard Viewer.

Press the Del key to clear the contents of the clipboard. In the Clear Clipboard message, click on Yes.

A clip art image, copied to the Clipboard

2 Click on File, Save As... to save the current contents of the clipboard as a .clp file.

Imaging

Imaging is a more advanced method of enhancing scanned images. You can also:

- work with a wider range of graphics file formats (including faxes)

- annotate images

> Click on Start. Move the mouse pointer over Programs, then Accessories. Click on Imaging.

Click on Open in the File menu and select a graphics file. Alternatively, click on New or Scan New... also from the File menu.

To edit the file, use the Annotation toolbar in the bottom lefthand corner of the screen – the tools are explained at the bottom of this page.

Annotation toolbar

To customise any of the toolbars, right-click any button.

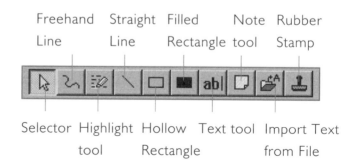

Freehand Line   Straight Line   Filled Rectangle   Note tool   Rubber Stamp

Selector   Highlight tool   Hollow Rectangle   Text tool   Import Text from File

Phone Dialer

This is a useful program, especially if you don't have a speed dial facility on your phone. Before you can use it though, you'll need a modem connected to your computer and it must be the type you can connect your phone into.

| Click on Start and move the mouse over Programs, then Accessories, Communications. Then click on Phone Dialer.

Click on the down-arrow to access previously dialled numbers.

To change or delete a Speed dial number, click on the Edit menu. Then click on Speed Dial...

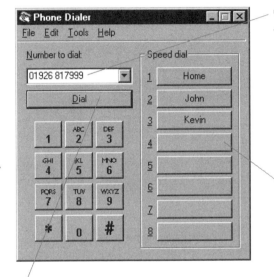

2 Type in the phone number or click on buttons below, simulating buttons on a phone.

Speed dialling

Click on one of the empty Speed dial buttons to program it.

3 Click on Dial.

4 Wait for the number to be dialled. When you hear a high pitched tone, follow the on-screen instructions.

5 Use your telephone as normal.

Standard settings

You can also access Dialing Properties by double-clicking on Telephony from the Control Panel.

Set your location, area code, outside line prefix, calling card to use when dialling long distance, etc.

| Click on Tools and then Dialing Properties...

Calculator

The Calculator provides both Standard and Scientific calculators.

1 Click on Start and move the mouse over Programs, then Accessories. Finally, click on Calculator.

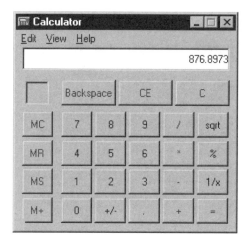

2 Click on the relevant buttons (similar to buttons on a hand-held calculator) or type the values from your keyboard.

3 To perform trigonometric and statistical functions, click on the View menu and then Scientific.

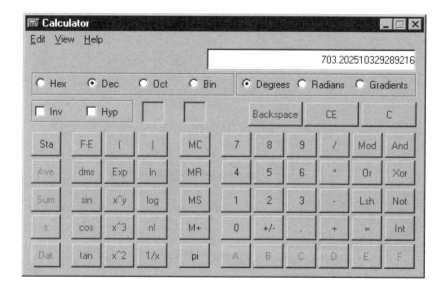

Maintaining your System

Windows ME includes a set of tools to enhance the performance and reliability of your PC. Use this chapter to ensure you continue to work efficiently and securely.

Covers

Chapter Thirteen

Displaying Disk Properties

As for other objects in Windows ME, you can easily access the Properties dialog box for a disk. Then, you can check general details about your disk, like the amount of free space available, and perform *housekeeping* routines like scanning your disk for errors and defragmenting it.

To format a floppy disk, right-click its icon in My Computer or Windows Explorer. Click on Format... in the shortcut menu. In the Format dialog, select Quick (to perform a rapid format if the disk has already been formatted before) or Full. Click on Start.

When the format is complete, click on Close twice.

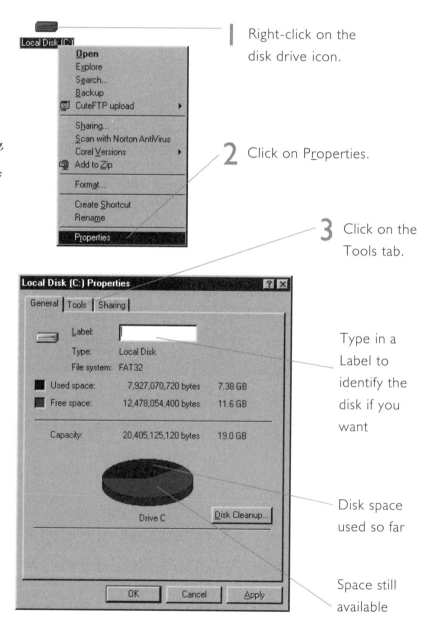

Right-click on the disk drive icon.

2 Click on Properties.

3 Click on the Tools tab.

Type in a Label to identify the disk if you want

Disk space used so far

Space still available

...cont'd

You can schedule ScanDisk and Defragmenter (or any other Windows program), see page 182.

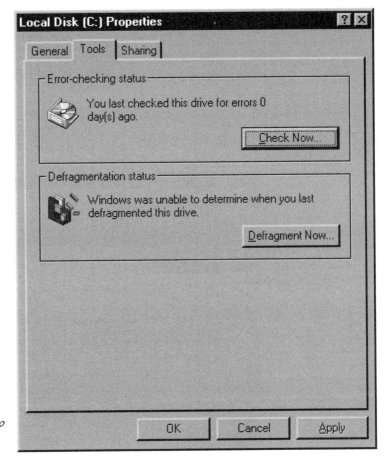

```
Local Disk (C:) Properties                      ? X

  General │ Tools │ Sharing │

  ┌─ Error-checking status ──────────────────────────┐
  │        You last checked this drive for errors 0   │
  │        day(s) ago.                                │
  │                              [ Check Now... ]     │
  └───────────────────────────────────────────────────┘

  ┌─ Defragmentation status ─────────────────────────┐
  │        Windows was unable to determine when you last │
  │        defragmented this drive.                   │
  │                              [ Defragment Now... ]│
  └───────────────────────────────────────────────────┘



            [ OK ]      [ Cancel ]      [ Apply ]
```

Another way to schedule disk maintenance activities is to use the Maintenance Wizard, see page 172.

Sharing tab	used to make a disk drive shareable so that other users can access it on a network (see page 132).
Check Now...	looks for disk errors and fixes them. See Scanning your Disk for Errors (next topic).
Defragment Now...	reorganises the disk to speed up file access. See Defragmenting your Disk (page 170).

Scanning your Disk for Errors

This is achieved by using a utility called ScanDisk. It allows you to analyse and repair problems with your disk. Although it's common to use ScanDisk on your main hard disk, you can also use it on any removable disks.

Windows will run ScanDisk automatically if you're starting your PC again after an improper shutdown.

| Click on ScanDisk from Start button, Programs, Accessories, System Tools or run it from Disk Properties.

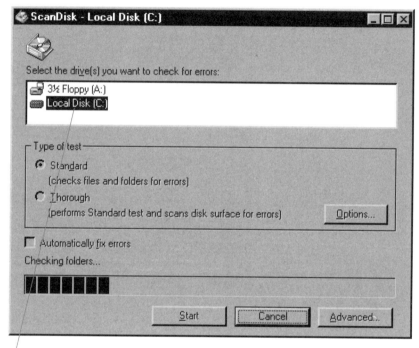

2 Click to highlight the disk to scan.

3 Choose options as explained below, then click on Start.

The Standard test will perform basic checks like looking for *Lost file fragments.* This is when over time files become fragmented on a disk (see Defragmenting your Disk), and so different parts are linked together by pointers. If these pointers are corrupted, then some parts of a file cannot be retrieved. ScanDisk can find these fragments and either delete them from the disk to free up space or create special files to write them into. You can try and recover the fragments lost from these files, but more often than not you'll not be successful.

Another standard check is for *cross-linked files*. This is when there are two pointers addressing the same file block. Pointers have to be unique so this condition is an error. It is worth opting to Make copies of the file block that has two pointers in the hope that at least one of the files can be rescued. Select this and other options from the Advanced... button.

The default options shown here are recommended.

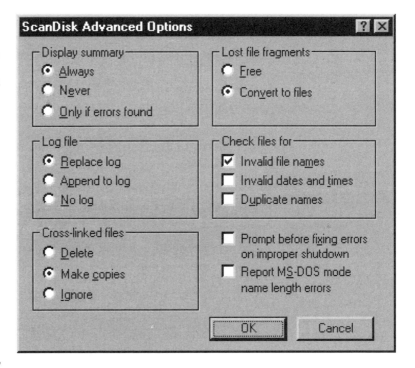

Although a Thorough scan takes longer, it's worth running it occasionally on your important disk.

The Thorough scan option performs a disk surface scan too. This reads and writes back each *cluster* (or allocation unit) on disk to ensure that there are no problems.

The surface scan can fix errors by trying to write data from *bad sectors* found on disk to another area on the disk.

Defragmenting your Disk

A file is not always stored in a single contiguous disk location. It may be split and stored in different areas of the disk, particularly if you are frequently updating and deleting your files. This fragmentation doesn't damage the files, but when you want to access them, it takes longer. This is because first of all, at the end of each file fragment, a pointer needs to be read to give the address of where the next fragment is stored on disk. Then, the disk heads may need to move to an entirely different part of the disk to retrieve the chained fragment. This process can continue depending on how fragmented a particular file has become, making the access inefficient and slow.

You can reorganise your disk so that each file stored (perhaps as several pieces scattered all over the disk) is read and then written back in continuous storage locations. This will speed up access to all your files when you need to use them again.

1 Click on Disk Defragmenter from Start button, Programs, Accessories, System Tools. Or run it from Disk Properties.

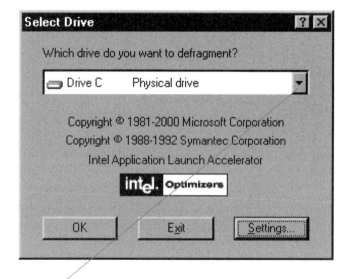

Click on Settings... to ensure that your program files are rearranged so that your programs start faster.

2 Select the drive. Then click on OK.

...cont'd

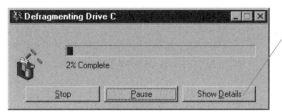

3 Click to see Disk Defragmenter working.

The time it takes to defragment your hard disk will depend on:

* *how fragmented it is*
* *its size*
* *the speed of your computer*

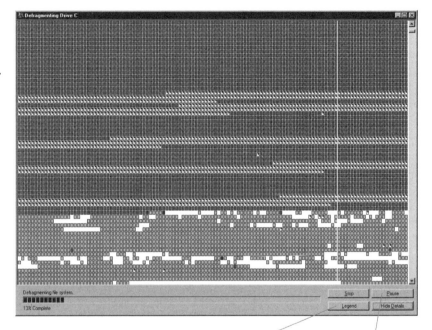

Click on the Legend button to see what the different coloured squares are.

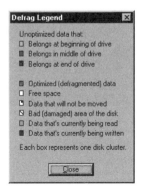

Click to temporarily pause the defragmenting. This will speed up other Windows programs you may be running at the same time.

Using the Maintenance Wizard

You can use a special wizard – the Maintenance Wizard – to:

- make your programs run faster (by running the Disk Defragmenter)

- troubleshoot your hard disk (by running ScanDisk)

- make more space available on your hard disk (by deleting unnecessary files e.g. temporary Internet and Windows files)

The Maintenance Wizard works by scheduling: you specify when it runs, and the operations it carries out. You can, however, also have Windows ME carry out the specified tasks at any time.

> | Click on Maintenance Wizard from Start button, <u>P</u>rograms, Accessories, System Tools.
>
> When you run the wizard for the first time, the dialog below does not launch. Instead, simply complete the dialogs which appear on the facing page.

Click here: then click on OK (omit steps 2–5) to have Windows perform preset maintenance tasks now.

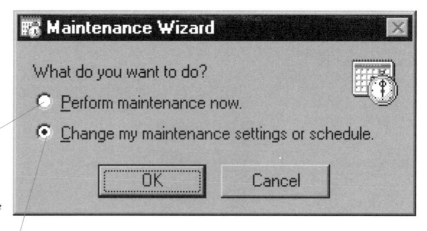

2 Click here. Then click on OK.

...cont'd

Select the Custom option (and complete the dialogs which launch) for more control over maintenance tasks. For instance, you can specify which programs run automatically when Windows ME starts, thereby reducing load time.

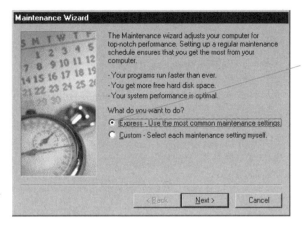

3 Click here. Then click on <u>N</u>ext.

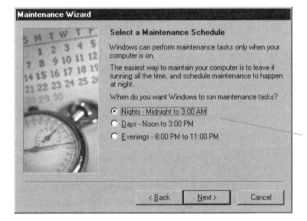

4 Select a scheduling period. Then click on <u>N</u>ext.

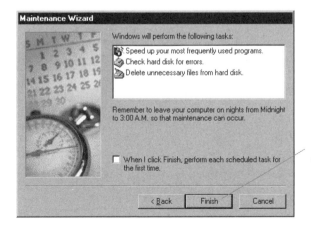

5 Click on Finish.

Cleaning Up Unnecessary Files

Use the Disk Cleanup utility to regain some disk space by removing the following kinds of transient Windows files:

- Temporary files

- Deleted files in the Recycle Bin

- Downloaded Internet programs

Click on Start, Programs, Accessories, System Tools. Then click on Disk Cleanup.

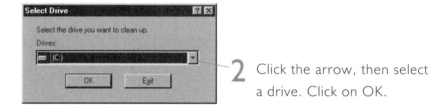

2 Click the arrow, then select a drive. Click on OK.

The total disk space you'll gain by deleting files in each category is shown on the right and the overall total space displayed at the top.

The View Files button will display all the files in a selected category.

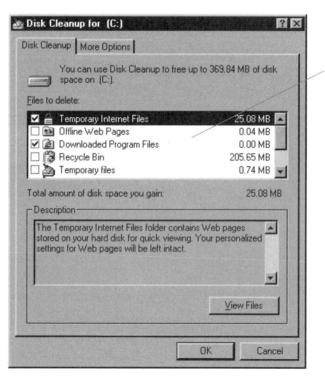

3 Select one or more categories (a tick appears in the box). Then click on OK.

To save even more disk space

The first two Clean up... buttons run Add/Remove Programs (as described on page 51).

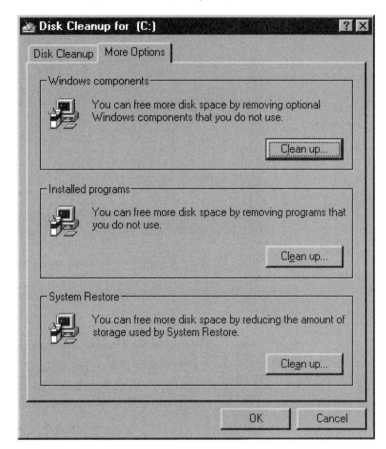

| Click on the More Options tab.

2 Click on the appropriate Clean up... button(s) to remove unused Windows components, other programs and space reserved by System Restore (see later) to save even more disk space.

Downloading Internet Updates

You can use Windows Update to download the latest drivers and system updates/enhancements, thus ensuring that your PC's Windows installation is always up-to-date.

You can also access the centralised Windows Update web site by pointing your browser to: http://windowsupdate. microsoft.com/

1 Click on Windows Update from the Start button.

2 Once connected online, click on the Product Updates link and then download the relevant components.

Windows Update also provides product assistance information.

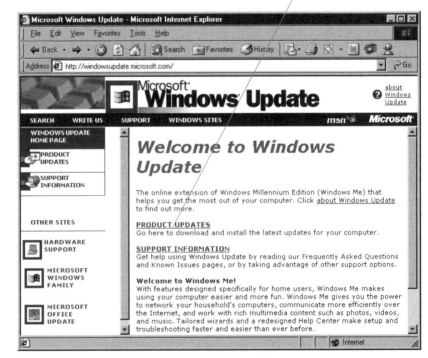

Automatic Updates setting

Windows ME is clever enough to decide for itself if your system needs to be updated and goes ahead online by itself if you let it. Luckily, you can change this default so that it'll notify you first before downloading any updates, or you can just manually look for new updates whenever you want to.

I Double-click on Automatic Updates from the Control Panel (Start, Settings, Control Panel).

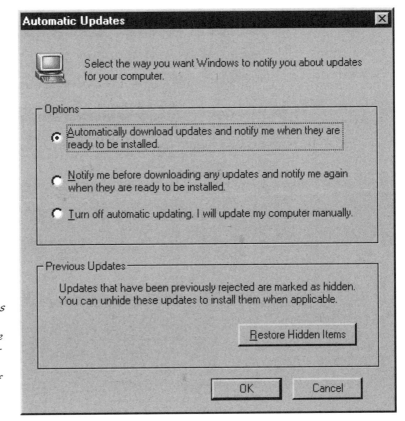

The Restore Hidden Items button ensures components rejected in the past for installation appear the next time Windows notifies you of updates – if they're still appropriate.

2 Change the Options as described above. Click OK.

Displaying System Information

Using the System Information utility, you can gather detailed configuration information about your hardware, system components and software in one convenient place. This provides a lot of technical data about the way your system is set up.

You can also access system information and alter settings by right-clicking on My Computer icon and choosing Properties.

In the illustration below, the System Information utility is supplying basic information about the sound card fitted.

Click on Start, Programs, Accessories, System Tools. Then click on System Information.

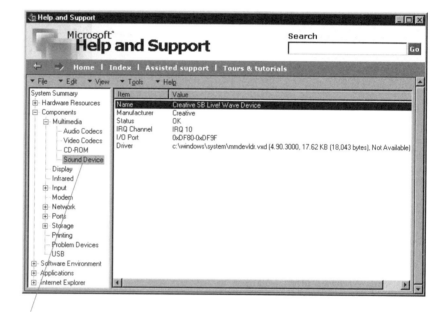

2 Click on an item to display the relevant details.

Other Views

Click on View and select Advanced. This shows all the information in the basic view plus additional information that may be useful to a advanced user or a technical support specialist. Click on System History (also from the View menu) to see details of changes after a specified date.

Saving System Information/System History

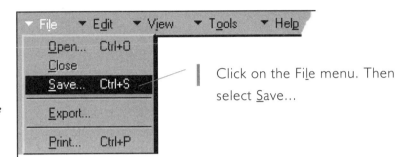

You can only open a .nfo file using System Information.

1 Click on the File menu. Then select Save...

2 Locate the folder you want to save the file into, name the file and then for the file type choose:

.NFO to save the current settings for your system, or

.XML to save the history of changes to your system

Use the Export... option to save the system information or system history to a text file. It can then be opened in any text editor and you can email it to a technical support contact to help you with troubleshooting.

System Tools

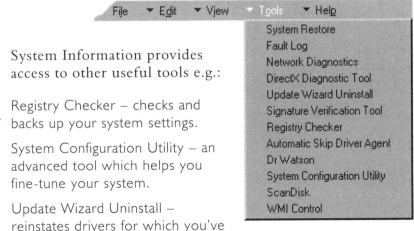

System Restore is covered on page 184.

System Information provides access to other useful tools e.g.:

Registry Checker – checks and backs up your system settings.

System Configuration Utility – an advanced tool which helps you fine-tune your system.

Update Wizard Uninstall – reinstates drivers for which you've installed updated versions.

Configuring Power Options

As long as your PC supports it you can save power by having Windows ME:

1. turn off your monitor.

2. turn off your hard disk.

3. put your PC on standby – turns off your monitor and hard disk (especially useful for portable computers).

4. make it hibernate – same as standby but also saves whatever's in memory at the time to your hard disk. So when you turn your PC back on, the memory state is loaded and you can just carry on from the point you left off.

You can specify the intervals at which these shutoffs occur. You can also save these setting combinations as 'power schemes', which makes applying them even easier.

Power Options settings

Control Panel is available from Start, Settings. If you can't locate the Power Options icon, click on view all Control Panel options link.

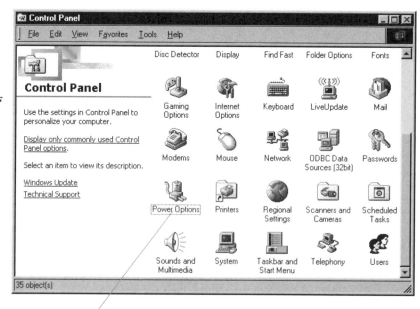

Double-click on Power Options from the Control Panel.

...cont'd

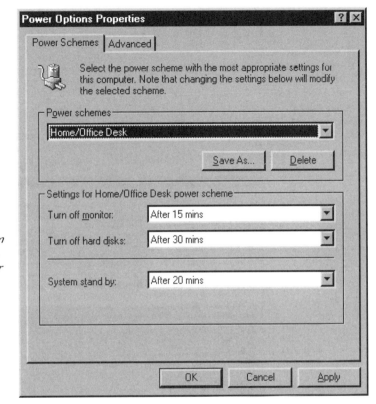

Instead of setting System stand by here, do it whenever you want to from when you go to Shut Down your PC (see page 24).

2 Click on Power schemes drop-down arrow to select a preset power scheme, or alter the settings below for the current scheme. Click on OK.

Creating a power scheme

1 After altering the settings above, click: Save As...

Click on the Delete button to delete the current power scheme.

2 Name the new scheme, then click on OK.

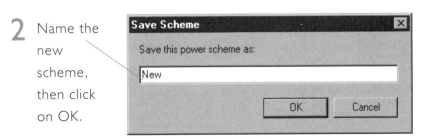

Scheduling Tasks

You can have any Windows program run automatically at the time and interval you specify.

Windows uses a special wizard – the Scheduled Task Wizard – to automate scheduling.

1 Click on Start, Programs, Accessories, System Tools, Scheduled Tasks.

2 Double-click on the Add Scheduled Task item.

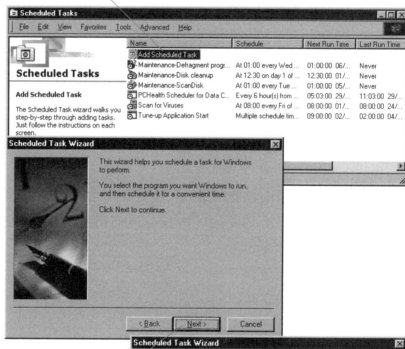

3 Click on Next.

Re step 4 - if the program you want to schedule isn't listed, click on the Browse... button to locate it.

4 Click on a program entry. Then click on Next.

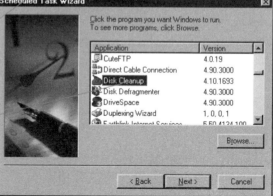

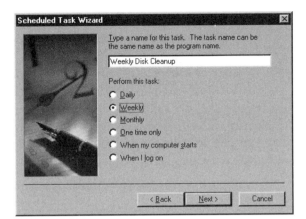

5 Amend the program name to a task name if necessary and decide when to perform the task.

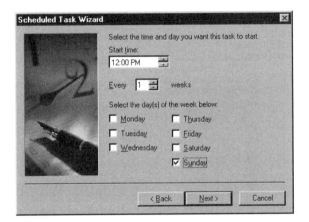

6 Set the time to perform the task. This box will depend on how often you perform the task in step 5.

After you've finished setting up a task, it appears in the Scheduled Task window (step 2). Right-click on it and choose Properties to alter any of it's settings (e.g. when it runs), or choose Delete to remove it.

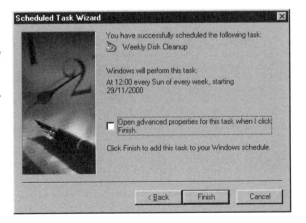

7 Review the summary of the scheduled task, clicking Back to change options. Then click on Finish.

Restoring your System

There are essentially three types of Restore points:

- *System checkpoints – these are automatic restore points created by Windows.*

- *Manual restore points – these are the ones you'll create before a major change to your system.*

- *Installation restore points – these are automatically created when certain programs are installed.*

In the past, when things went wrong with Windows it was very hard, even for an experienced user, to get the system working normally again. Now a new feature called System Restore resolves this problem. It monitors the changes made to Windows over time (like when you add new programs and hardware) by taking a snapshot at regular intervals of your setup. Then, if you experience problems with Windows, you can use System Restore to "roll back" to an earlier setup that did work properly.

1   Click on Start, Programs, Accessories, System Tools, System Restore.

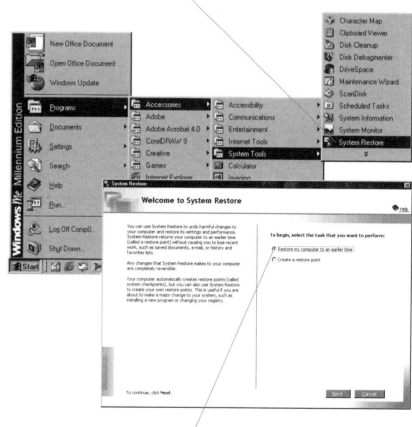

System Restore has to reserve some of your hard disk space for it to work. You can change this allocation by right-clicking on My Computer, clicking on Properties, Performance tab, File System... button.

You can set up System Restore to run as a scheduled task, as described on page 182.

2   Select 'Restore my computer to an earlier time' option and then click Next.

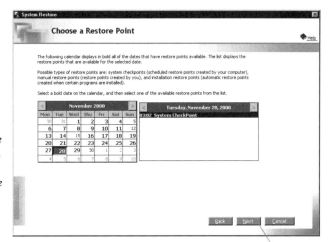

 If you choose the option 'Create a restore point' in step 2, it will be marked on the calendar here as a bold date.

3 Select a bold date from the calendar (use arrows to go back and forth), and then a specific restore point. Click on Next.

4 Ensure all your files and programs are closed, then click OK.

5 Confirm the restore point by clicking on Next.

6 Windows will display a Restoring in Progress dialog and then restart your system.

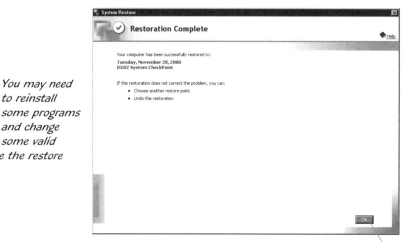

You may need to reinstall some programs and change some valid settings since the restore point.

7 After Windows restarts you should see a successfully restored message. Click OK.

Undoing a Restoration

Instead of Undoing a Restoration, you may decide to just restore to another point.

To begin, select the task that you want to perform:

○ Restore my computer to an earlier time

○ Create a restore point

◉ Undo my last restoration

If you've just done a restore and things haven't improved with your system, you can Undo the last restoration. Simply run System Restore again and select the option to Undo, created there automatically by Windows.

Index

B

C

D

N

O

P